For Dona Nelson

With
love
and
all good wishes

Wyatt Cooper
Natchez
June 2 '77

FAMILIES

FAMILIES

A Memoir and a Celebration

Wyatt Cooper

Harper & Row, Publishers

New York, Evanston,

San Francisco, London

Grateful acknowledgment is made to Mediarts, Inc. for permission to reprint lines from the song "American Pie," written by Don McLean. Copyright © 1971 Mayday Music, Inc., Yahweh Tunes, Inc.

Portions of this work originally appeared in *Town & Country* magazine.

FIRST EDITION

Designed by Janice Willcocks Stern

Library of Congress Cataloging in Publication Data

Cooper, Wyatt.
    Families: a memoir and a celebration.
    1. Cooper family. 2. Cooper, Wyatt. I. Title.
CS71.C777   1975   929'.2'0973   75-9347
ISBN 0-06-010857-6

75 76 77 78 79 10 9 8 7 6 5 4 3 2 1

To my two families,
the one that made me
and the one I made

CONTENTS

Illustrations

Foreword

As far as its author is concerned a book is never completed. It is simply abandoned. Things continue to happen in his life; changes occur, and he feels the need to include them.

In September, 1974, as I was about to end this book, I went with my wife and sons to Quitman, Mississippi, to visit the farm where I grew up. My nine-year-old son Carter had often asked to see the place where my life began. Seven-year-old Anderson was looking forward to catching some fish from the pond on the land that had nurtured my family for generations. I had often, in my imagination, brought them together before this, the yesterday and the tomorrow of my life, the landscape that figures vividly in my memories and the two little boys who represent my involvement in the future, and I felt impelled, before turning loose these pages, to introduce one to the other in fact.

As we drove out from Quitman in a heavy downpour, I reminded the children that the place would not look as I had described it. I knew that the house and barns were gone, the well filled in, and the land untilled and untenanted, but I was unprepared for what we found. Even the road was not where it had been. No trace remained of the house I had known and loved. Where the peach orchard had been, where the cotton fields had been, the pasture, the blackberry patches, the fences—all had been swallowed up by time. A forest of tall pine trees covered the entire 260 acres, and it seems a strange irony to me that the sale of timber brings in more income than all the cotton we ever grew.

I was born there in 1927 and the land, then, provided our total living. We lived on it much as my grandparents had before us, with independence and self-reliance and pride, and our wants were modest. Our transportation was still the horse and buggy, and my first lessons were at the same one-room schoolhouse that my mother had attended. Back then, I once asked my father what we could get for our farm if we sold it and he said "about three thousand dollars." Today, I am told, it is worth something like a quarter of a million dollars, and everybody says it would be foolish to let it go, for oil wells are being drilled all around it.

The town itself had grown, but in essence it remained unchanged. The Confederate soldier, high on his monument in front of the Clarke County Courthouse, still gazed down Main Street. We walked along the street, my family and I, and went into the stores, where I found the familiar friends I had known. What had not survived elsewhere survived in the warmth of their welcomes and embraces. One woman, old now, but not old when I knew her, looked at my sons and said, "Lord, Buddy, it's like seeing you starting all over again."

We went to Meridian, where I lived during my eighteenth and nineteenth years. We stopped at the radio station where I had worked at that time as an announcer. We looked at the house my mother had lived in and we visited her grave in Magnolia Cemetery. Most of my connections with that city are gone now, and I thought that years would pass before I returned.

But two months later, just after I handed in the first draft of these pages, Elsie, the youngest of my five sisters, suffered a heart attack and I was called to Atlanta. At the airport, as I wrote the date on the check with which I purchased a ticket, I realized that it was her thirty-eighth birthday. She died two weeks later and my wife and I made one more sad journey to Mississippi to bury her.

In a large family one grows familiar with death. One loses grandparents, uncles, aunts, and parents, but it usually happens in the ripeness of age and can be seen as the closing off of a rich, full life. With Elsie, it was the loss of youth, of a promise unfulfilled, the end of a life not yet lived. She was sweet and vulnerable and gifted with a quick and curious mind, with an appetite for life and for growth. She had not begun to leave off learning. Her death seemed so unlikely a thing, so impossible to take in, that it was a numbed and unbelieving group that came together in Meridian, traveling, some of us, from the distant cities to which our lives and work have removed us. Elsie's husband, Harlan Luke, and their sixteen-year-old son and nineteen-year-old daughter brought her body from Atlanta. Marie came from Hartford, Connecticut, Janice from Miami, Harry from La Jolla, California, and Preston from Hartford. Annie Laura, the eldest of us, and a great-grandmother, lives in Quitman still. Grace, who was, at seventeen, my teacher at the schoolhouse I mentioned, lives nearby in Forest. This parting, more than my mother's death two years before, marked the real breaking up of the family circle. Never again will all eight of us be together at Christmas, gathered around the fireside that meant home, all of us talking at once, laughing at old jokes, retelling old stories, showing off our children, and rejoicing in our shared experiences.

There comes a time in the history of families when the scorekeepers are gone, and no one is left who acts as a central clearing place, keeps the records, maintains the lines of contact. The time comes when we go back only for funerals. At the wake on the night before the burial, the familiar faces appear, some of them changed, and some of them, having changed, remaining the same. There is a breathless moment of recognition. We smile our child's smile, for we are briefly children again, then we hold each other close and weep onto each other's shoulders.

Then we straighten up and talk of other matters. We tell funny stories about our children. We laugh together and we remember many things.

In the days since Elsie died tender memories of her crowd into my mind. I remember her at four, when she had straight and stringy hair at a time when Shirley Temple's curly mop was still the ideal. She was also bad-tempered; she went around in boy's overalls and carried a hammer that she was not above using as a weapon if she felt that she had been slighted. I decided that her unhappiness stemmed from her feelings about her hair, so I took her to Quitman on the school bus and for $1.00 got her a permanent wave. She came out of the beauty shop with her hair in a thousand ringlets and a radiant smile on her face. By the time it grew out, Margaret O'Brien had become the rage. Elsie and I hurried to each of her movies; we put her hair into pigtails like those of little Miss O'Brien, and we were both overjoyed when strangers commented on her resemblance to the star. Her disposition from that time on was never to be less than sunny. I remember a special evening in Atlanta a few years back when Elsie and her family took me to a restaurant that featured country cooking of the kind we grew up on, such as black-eyed peas, turnip greens, and corn bread. A black woman moved among the tables singing songs that were familiar to us from our childhood. She stopped at our table and began to sing "Amazing Grace," a great and moving hymn that we had sung a hundred times at Pleasant Grove Baptist Church. Elsie and I looked at each other and laughed, for each of us knew what would happen to the other; we held hands and cried disgracefully.

She had been excited about this book; as I worked on it, I read certain passages from it to her over the telephone, and it was at her urging that I included some comments on the fear of Hell, for she and I once sat up and talked through the night about the cruel and debilitating effect of that fear, and afterward I sent her a copy of a sixteenth-century epitaph:

Here lie I, Martin Elginbrodde;
Have mercy on my soul, Lord God;
As I wad do, were I Lord God
And ye were Martin Elginbrodde.

When I told her that I was going to include that epitaph in the book, it made her laugh.

I also remember that she ended all our telephone conversations with a soft, almost shy, declaration, "I love you."

The days that followed her death were, for me, overcast by a terrible pall of sadness, a kind of perplexity that could not be shaken off. But Christmas came, and, with it, the drawing together of my own little family group. There was the familiar joy of the children, their delight in the new bicycles they had themselves picked out, the presence of Stan and Chris, my stepsons, now fine young adults, and the splendid painting that my wife, knowing the pleasure I take in her art, had made for me. Christmas is also our anniversary. This one was our eleventh, and to mark the occasion, she painted a family portrait. The setting is our living room; in it, she and I and our two boys form a continuing circle that is complete, comforting, sweet, and durable; that seems inviolate, hopeful, and, somehow, sacred.

New York City
December 27, 1974

1

Of Sons and Immortality

*"One generation passeth away, and another genera-
tion cometh: but the earth endureth for ever."*
—*Ecclesiastes 1:4*

*"As a little childe riding behind his father, sayde sim-
ply unto him, Father, when you are dead, I shal ride
in the Saddle."*   —STEFANO GUAZZO

One day, when Carter was three years old, he asked me, "When
I get to be as old as you are now, will you be very old and getting
ready to die?"

Something turned over in my stomach; my eyes burned; and
I felt a constriction in my throat. He had asked an elemental
question. It deserved as honest and as simple an answer as I could
give so I said "Yes." I will be, if I am alive, in my eighties, and
I told him what I hope and believe to be the truth, that if I have
lived that long I will have known much of the joys and rewards
of living; I will have seen him and his brother embarked well into
their lives, and I can expect to turn loose with some feeling that
the more important part of me will live on in them and in their
children and in their children's children. He could accept that,
and, after some thoughtful shaking of his head, he returned to his
play.

He had begun trying to understand the fact of death some time
earlier. After seeing the movie *Ben-Hur* he asked one day, "All

1

that was two thousand years ago?" I answered, "Yes." ". . . And all the people who were alive then are dead now?" Again, "Yes." ". . . And lots of people have been born since then and then got old and died?" "Yes." ". . . And someday everybody alive now will be dead and there will be other people living here?" "Yes." There was no other answer to give. He had summed the whole story up very well. He thought it over for a few moments and he rendered a judgment. "It's a strange way of doing it," he said.

Well, he's not the first one in history to whom that thought has occurred, but he came to a conclusion, accepted it, and could get on with his life in the light of that knowledge. It might not be exactly as he would have desired it, but he could see sense in it. It might not be as I would have arranged it if I had been making man, but there it is, the central fact of our lives. Sooner or later we learn to live with it. It may be our tragedy or it may be precisely that truth that gives our lives the meaning, the significance, and the perspective that they have. The accommodation we make with our knowledge of the transient nature of time may be the single heroic element in our lives.

If an endless vista of days stretched forever ahead of us, it might be that we would have no reason to prize the one we are passing through, just as one does not know how to relish happiness until one has known some sorrow. Our parents lived in a greater intimacy with death. They knew it as a specter that waited around every turn of the road, and as such they came to terms with it. We have in our time generally succeeded in denying its existence. We try to look the other way for as long as possible. We avoid the dying and we dress up the dead as if it were all a pretty fiction. It seems to me to be a matter of some importance that we accept the fact that our lives will have an end, that, further, we will change from year to year, from day to day, and that each space of time in our lives has its own reality and its own reason, its own rigors and its own rewards.

I cherish each day with my children, for never again will that little boy be the same little boy he is today. He may indeed grow daily in splendor, and each new stage will have its delights, but he will not be the same; therefore I must enjoy today's child today. Never again will Carter be exactly that same brave little soldier he was one day when he was three and I looked out my window and saw him on the way to the park with his nurse and his baby brother. Carter was dressed in full Roman armor, with a red plume bobbing from his helmet, and his cardboard sword was thrust fearlessly forward as if defying the world, every ounce of his plump little frame leaning into the future, eager and pushing for adventure, while his other hand held tightly onto the safety of the nurse's skirt.

That was yesterday, and today he is already a tall young man of dignity and poise, with a love of books, of places and of people, and with opinions and thoughts of his own. Anderson can still without embarrassment run and jump into my arms, throw his arms tightly around my neck and squeeze with loving abandon. He can crawl into my lap, curl up like a puppy, and fall asleep against me. Tomorrow, or the day after, or the year after that, he will be a grave young man, solemnly shaking hands, keeping his secrets to himself, and expressing his love for me only with a quick and laughing eye or with an impulsive seizing of my hand.

In the meantime one treasures each moment, preserves it, locks it away in memory, and knows that what exists between us tomorrow will be based on the joy, the respect, the truth, and the love that are ours today.

Our lives are like that. What exists at the end is the sum total of what our single days have been.

To escape death, to cheat its cruel annihilation, we build monuments to ourselves; we establish empires; we collect memorabilia, accumulate clutter; we make books; we write our names in the sand; we leave little signs saying "I was here." But our real survival, the only immortality we can be sure of, is that part of ourselves we invest in others, the contribution we make to the totality of man, the knowledge we have shared, the truths we have found, the causes we have served, the lessons we have lived. Our accumulated faults and virtues, frailties and strengths—these we hand down.

I see myself in my two sons. In their youth, their promise, their possibilities, my stake in immortality is invested. I look in the mirror these days and it is my father's face that stares back at me. It is a part of the process of becoming an ancestor. I hear those tender and stalwart little men asking the questions I asked and am still asking, and I watch them wrestling with the answers with which I wrestled and still wrestle. There is a visible and awesome splendor in the constancy of their growth, in the expansion of their grasp, in the continuing extension of their world. In it I see the saga of mankind in miniature. The sight and sound of it move me, as music, poetry, beauty, logic, and love move me, as life moves me.

In their rise is my decline. They will be able to jump fences that I will no longer have the will or the call to jump. They will run races that I did not run. Win competitions, perhaps, that I never dared to enter. There is rightness in that. There are hope and triumph in it, and it seems good to me. I can help. I can play a part in giving them some of the equipment they will need, something of courage and understanding, something of what I have learned, something of what I am.

Twice it has been my joy to stand and look with awe and reverence and hope into the face of a newborn son. There is always some astonishment at the ever-recurring miracle of birth; like the coming of the green each spring, it always surprises and it always humbles.

The question mark and promise and wild possibility that exist in each newborn infant are a reminder to us of that in ourselves which is godlike—godlike in reason, in apprehension, and in vision. It hangs above the cradle like a rainbow. There are magic and mystery in that frail bundle of flesh. He has genius in his tiny head. He can grow and he can learn. The beauty of the world is in his face; he sleeps with the innocence of snow; he rages with the authority of Jove; and his brave little flower of a fist will grow to hold the plow, drive the ships, heal the sick, sway the multitudes, and perhaps even point the way to a happier new world.

And there is always the glorious possibility that from the young, from their re-examining, their rediscovering, their re-experiencing, from their new inspirations and new insights, will come a strengthening of man's probabilities. There may come some new energy, some new sweetness, some new revelation. I want to feel that some part of the best of me will remain, like a grain of sand on a wide clean beach, in that possibly better world.

This hope is not new with me. It has always been man's vision and from it has come that long march of progress from our beginnings. Because of it he has created various systems for the transmission of knowledge from one age to another, but the principal instrument through which the piled-up wisdoms, instincts, skills, and acquisitions of customs have traditionally been passed on, generation to generation, has been the ancient institution of the family. It seems to me that upon the survival of that family depends not only the individual's hope of immortality but the very future of the race.

They Say the Family Is Finished

"The thing that hath been, it is that which shall be;
and that which is done is that which shall be done; and
there is no new thing under the sun."
—Ecclesiastes 1:9

They are saying these days that the family is finished, at least as we have known it. That's a sad and lonely thought. I suppose they may even be right. Everything passes. Other venerable institutions have vanished. Civilizations fall. Worlds end. Gods, even, have died and are dying, so there is no real reason to think that anything lasts forever.

Still, for most of us, whatever the stress and strain contained therein, it was from the warmth, support, and security of the family nest that we first looked out with wonder at the universe. It was there we began to unravel the puzzle of ourselves, of other people, and of the world around us. It was in the shelter of that family that we first glimpsed the complexity of life. It was from the fortress of that circle that we ventured forth to experiment and explore, and back to it that we fled when fears and failures affronted us. There seeds were planted. There our characters were formed, our destinies shaped. There we were to learn almost all we would ever know of loving.

I do not like to think of a society in which there are no families. Already in our time we have seen the family diminished from what it was in our youth, a large, unwieldy clan of vastly differing personalities welded inseparably together by the bond of blood, to today's claustrophobic units of two, three, or four persons who seem to have no outside kin and no antecedents. In my day we had grandparents, sometimes great-grandparents; aunts; uncles; cousins, once, twice and even three times removed; relatives of all sizes, shapes, and dispositions, of all sorts and conditions, of every age from the ancient and dying to the yearly fresh crop of babies. The similarities and resemblances among us, or the lack of them, were discussed, analyzed, and compared, as were our virtues and our failings. It was agreed, for instance, that my nose and my conceit were pure Cooper but that my coloring and my quiet manner came from the Andersons, my mother's people. I was considered lucky to have inherited a head shaped like that of Grandpa Cooper—it stuck out behind something like the back end of an old-fashioned hammer. I shared this inheritance with only one of the dozens of Cooper cousins, and it was assumed that with it went Grandpa's brilliant mind. We were, accordingly, expected to do the family some credit. In the case of my cousin, Frank Rose, the assumptions found fulfillment, either because there was something to the idea to start with or because the expectations spurred him on to notable achievement. In high school he was already dazzling; as good-looking as anybody you'd ever want to have around, as popular as a movie star, a top athlete and a top scholar, he was elected president of any campus organization he happened to saunter near. By the time he was twenty-nine he was president of a college, and later performed brilliantly as President of the University of Alabama during years of intense crisis. *Time* and *Life* magazines might have been impressed, but there was nothing remarkable about it to my aunts. To them the honors paid him had nothing to do with hard work, clever planning, or diligent study. It was just Grandpa's head, that's all. With that head, what did you expect? As for me—well, my head never did jut out as far as Frank's anyway.

Families banded together in those days; they were curious

about each other and involved with each other. We knew where our ancestors were buried; we took care of their graves and we kept alive their stories. We attended each other's births, graduations, weddings, operations, and funerals. We had regular reunions and we visited each other in between.

The Andersons assembled yearly in the spring at Grandma's house. It was, of course, Grandpa's house too, but one spoke of it as "going to Grandma's," for she was the star of that establishment, the center around which the family revolved. If we went to my father's family, on the other hand, it was "going to Grandpa's," for there Grandpa Cooper was the undisputed ruler and Grandma faded into the background. (Few, indeed, managed much shine in his presence.)

Grandma Anderson was bright and witty, gay and original. Her conversation was quick and lively, and she had a great store of charm, with a country woman's frankness, even earthiness in a warm sort of way, and Grandpa was content to leave the talking to her; he sat and whittled—he was constantly making something —not always comfortable in company or totally approving of the boisterousness of all those grandchildren spilling over the house and yard. He was a deacon in the Baptist church, a good, decent, hard-working man with no sense of frivolity. His prayers at meals went beyond the simple obligation of saying grace, and though he mumbled through them in the manner of a modest man not wishing to call undue attention to himself or to intrude too firmly on the time of a busy deity, they were nonetheless fully meant and fully felt.

I remember hearing him say once that he believed the Lord had never seen fit to send him material success because he might not then have served Him as devotedly. That is as good a reason as any, I suppose, for being content with your lot in life, which he was. He was a carpenter and was available, once his crop was in, for the building of houses, barns, or other necessities. Grandma, though, was made of livelier stuff; she had a great sense of fun and engaged in a certain amount of horseplay; she would have been quite at home in any class at any time and in any place. His devotion to her was total, and when she died, he became even more silent and increasingly withdrawn until a few months later when he quietly followed her.

Everyone brought food to these reunions, so much that once the remainder was carted home again, we all lived off it through the following weeks. Those who came some distance arrived in automobiles stuffed full of Anderson descendants, with everybody holding baskets of food on their laps. After the clamor of greetings, with hugs and kisses and patting of backs and heads and noisy exchanging of extravagant compliments, there would be much hustling, bustling, and cheerful fussing as the white-cloth-covered dishes were unloaded. "Now you be careful with that roast, Bubber—Maggie Sue, go help him with that before he spills it right out on the ground." There would be cries of praise and protestations of astonishment as new offerings were brought forth; the bulk and variety of it (if not the taste) would have delighted the ancient Romans. "I can't wait to get my fork in Little Bit's banana puddin'!" "My, my, there's one of Little Sis's coconut cakes!"

There would be an army of fried chickens, Virginia hams, potato salad, blackberry pies, huckleberry pies, vanilla puddings, devil's food cakes, angel food cakes—in the matter of cakes a general ratio of one cake per person seemed to have been aimed at, and arrived at too, for that matter, and everything was fried in butter or fat and (my wife says) had sugar poured all over it. Such cooking ruins country people's palates forever, I suppose. I have absolutely no taste for fine food. The best French restaurants in the world are wasted on me. All I want is a few ham hocks fried in bacon grease, a little mess of turnips with sowbelly in it, and a hunk of corn bread and I'm happy.

Those were joyous occasions for me. To see all those colorful people of such variety gathered in holiday mood, with their jokes and their laughter and their familiarity with each other, was as exciting a thing as I knew. It was better than Christmas. They were my kin. We were of the same blood and bone. I felt related. They belonged to me, and we had claims on one another. Then there were all the cousins, many of them my age, and we could run all over the farm, matching skills and heights and strengths, testing each other, sharing opinions, pooling our knowledge of sex, comparing accounts of our various schools, the relative severities of our various teachers, and, with a little exaggeration, the excellence of our grades. The girls seemed prettier, more mysterious, than the ones we knew in school. With many of us, the first time we fell in love, it would be with a cousin—Bobby Joyce Raspberry, for instance. We could visit the spring under the hill where water for Grandma's house came from, and we could wade in the stream that ran from it. We could ignore our mother's warnings about not getting our good clothes dirty, and we could climb trees and get into fights. The older girls, the teenagers (though we did not then use the term), stood around in bunches, trying to act like young ladies, but whispering and tittering and going off into sudden, uncontrollable fits of giggling.

In the kitchen the women cooked, scraped, and consolidated, pouring sugar into pitchers of iced tea, checking the wrappings on the treasured block of ice brought dripping all the way from Quitman tied by ropes to the back bumper of the car, now worried over and speculated about—it must last through the making of the tea and into the afternoon, when it would freeze the ice cream, while we, the youngest, would sit on the freezer or take turns at the crank.

My aunts, Jewell Smith and Addie Flowers, came with their families from Laurel. They had a city look, with beads and earrings and makeup—Aunt Jewell with her high cheekbones, her light reddish hair and fair skin, and Aunt Addie with her china-blue eyes, her prematurely graying hair, her pretty girlish dresses and her flirtatious girlish manners. Aunt Lizzie Dearman lived up the road from us; her son, Willie Earl, was my friend; we played, went fishing, and roamed the woods together. Aunt Lizzie had a lovely, touching, face, vulnerable and smiling. She had buried three of her babies and there was a mark of sadness on her. Uncle Walter and Aunt Sadie came from Meridian. They had two sons, who were roughly my age, and the high point of my year came when I was allowed to spend a week with them in Meridian. There was, in their house, a sense of decorum and good behavior often missing in my own. They never raised their voices against each other and Uncle Walter never seemed to fall into those temper fits that were too familiar a part of my life with my father.

Aunt Lelia would have traveled from Stonewall; she had (and has) a dry, self-directed humor with some element in it of cheerful complaint, an element of complaint that was certainly justified, for she has had, all her life, one major illness after another. She has had more operations on more sections of the body than anyone I've ever heard of, and yet she has had the determination and strength of will to survive them all. Her husband was a strange-looking man much older than she, with a bent, angular frame, oddly intense dark eyes and a tendency to weep. She called him Mr. Raspberry, and so did we, since that was his name. He was of the Pentecostal persuasion, a religion that encourages the speaking of unknown tongues and seizures of shouting in a kind of divine ecstasy. At one of these family gatherings Mr. Raspberry got a bit carried away after lunch and began to shout, "Glory to God; we've all been spared another year . . ." and other such sentiments while tears rolled down his face. I asked my grandmother why Mr. Raspberry cried so much and she said, "Oh, if you ask me his bladder's just located too close to his eyes." That will give you an idea of Grandma. Another story: Once Grandma was complaining about the ugliness of some woman who had been visiting around in the area. Grandma and her daughters were all beauties, and, as beauties have a tendency to do, they set great store by physical attractiveness. Somebody said, "But, Mrs. Anderson, she can't help being ugly." Grandma said, "I know she can't help being ugly, but she could stay at home."

Sometimes some of her brothers would be there. The Campbell men were tall, with hairy arms and with eyes for the ladies. Uncle Bob Campbell, married to my grandfather's sister, Aunt Becky, was big in singing circles; he would travel miles to attend the all-day sings that country churches used to hold in those times. He would go and lead the singing, practice his manners, and squeeze ladies by the arm. Aunt Becky, being unmusical, was left at home.

Uncle Woodrow Wyatt would have a bottle stashed in his car, and to the grim disapproval of the wives, some of the men would from time to time slip the bottle out and wander down behind the barn with it. By late afternoon several of them would be showing its effect. They would abandon their game of pitching silver dollars and pile into the car with Uncle Woodrow. He would roar off down those country roads, sending up clouds of dust, scattering chickens and terrifying the animals of neighboring farms, while the men passed the bottle around again. When we saw the car returning—we could see it, across the cotton fields, when he made the turn over by the schoolhouse—there would be calls for Aunt Dora: "Dora, Dora, get out here! He's coming back," and Aunt Dora would run into the yard and stand with her back to the road pretending to chat casually with some member of the family. This was to demonstrate that she was not angry, that she was in fact hardly aware that he was tearing dangerously around the countryside, a menace to public safety. If her act was convincing, he would stop; if not, he kept going, and could be stopped, finally, only when Grandma and all the women stood beside the road waving gaily.

When the sun sank low in the west, we would begin to depart. Children would be tired and quarrelsome; some of us at least, having stayed too long at Little Bit's banana puddin', would be throwing up. The journeys home were not without dangers; cars broke down then, roads were not always reliable. Somebody would be trying to persuade Uncle Woodrow, speaking gently to avoid the hint of insult, that he should go to sleep on the back seat and let Aunt Dora take the wheel for the trip home. We went our separate ways with some sadness, for death used to strike often in those days when hospitals were very far away from some of us and medical care was primitive and slow. Sometimes it came like a bolt of lightning, without warning: a sudden attack of appendicitis, a child with pneumonia, and overnight someone was gone. Our departures, our farewells, our admonitions to each other to stay well, had more than ritual in them.

These reunions were of major importance to us. They registered the changes that took place in our lives: the marriages, the births, the moves, the prosperings and the failures to prosper. We watched each other growing up or growing old, and we felt ourselves to be a part of some timeless process, a process the rules of which applied equally to us all.

The reunions did not end when Grandma died, though they had already begun to fade some years before when she, like most of us, left her farm and moved to the town. It would never be the same in the city; there would be other demands upon one's attention; one would go as one went to other engagements; it became an event sandwiched in between other events.

One needs land, really, to feel that kind of sense of family, for in those days it was the land that made you, that nourished you, that would, eventually, claim you. The land was home. It was permanent and eternal; it had always been there and would always be there; it was made of the bones of millions of years and the dust of centuries; it had known the games of Indian boys, and the battles of unnamed men. You stretched out your body upon it in the early days of spring. You felt it grow warm beneath your belly. You filled your lungs with its clean, rich, and lusty smell. You ran hungry fingers through the tender green stubble of its surface; you lay and listened to the music of its silence, and gazed through half-closed eyes at the wide, high, pure, blue sky. It belonged to you and you belonged to it. You used it, you worked with it and upon it, but it stayed while you came and went, and whatever cities you might go to live in or work in or move through, you would remember that the land was waiting and you would return to it. The water would still flow from the spring; the grass would still grow in the pasture; mockingbirds would still nest in the pear tree by the barn. The young pines would grow tall, and the apple trees would grow old, but the land would live and give living to those who loved it.

After my grandparents had died we would still come together from time to time. My aunts in Laurel would dispatch letters all around the nation, to this group in Texas, that one in California, another in Maine, and we would assemble with our cars full of food on Aunt Addie's vast lawn in Laurel; but the intervals became wider and wider as the family spread farther and farther apart and deeper into the generations, and, of course, each time we gathered, we counted our losses. There are hundreds of us by now, and when we meet we are largely a company of strangers. Introductions are necessary, and there are many faces that are not familiar. The last one I went to was more than ten years ago. Uncle Bob Campbell was there, though at the age of ninety-three he would not last much longer. He sat in the shade of a tree and spoke spryly to all the young girls. "Your mother—" he would say to each one, though it is doubtful that he had a very clear idea just who any one of them was—"your mother was one of the most popular girls in her community." Late in the afternoon he had grown tired, and the sun, having shifted, had found its way through the branches of the tree he sat under, and a ray of light was shining in his face. Trying to move his face away from the light, and yet not sure what was bothering him, he mumbled to himself, "Up to now, I've had a good time."

Sometimes, in those days, we were proud of one of us and sometimes we were mortified, but always we followed each other's adventures. Each family had its constantly shifting currents and cross-currents, where each day's tide brought new conflicts and new subtleties. Each family with its layers of relationships had drama enough, color enough, passion enough, and provocation enough to fill all the stages of the world. Inside the circle of the extended family lived characters enough to people an epic, and, for some of us, that is exactly what they did. Again and again, when one came to know the world's literature, one found in Homer, Shakespeare, Dickens, and Tolstoy echoes of the same heroes, heroines, and villains that populated one's youth. Not only the characters in fiction, but also the people I've met in real life, I have found myself cataloguing in terms of these first people I knew in the community of Pleasant Grove, Mississippi.

I think of them as larger than life, as essences. Helen of Troy will always have Regina Armstead's face; pretty, pampered, frozen and spoiled, that face, prized by old Mrs. Armstead as if it were a precious jewel, set by accident on her daughter's neck, to be cared for, worried over, regarded as an investment in the future, looked upon as a ticket to the world outside, a possible passport to prosperity, not only for its possessor but for the mother as well. Regina was a sort of guardian of that face; the face was her reason for existing, the central preoccupation of her life. She carried it around as if it were a thing apart, separate from her, a banner and a mask, and she tried to talk through it, or around it; when she had to laugh, or feed herself, she tried to do it without disturbing any of its contours. Helen must have been like that.

God will always look like old Uncle Jesse Redmond, a veteran of the Civil War, a skeleton with a dirty white beard and burning little eyes darting around in an unmoving head; old Uncle Jesse, with his deafness, his testiness, his quick irritability, and his habit of dropping off in the middle of a sentence. An invisible circle seemed to have been drawn around him and one crossed it with slow and careful movements, calling attention to and defining one's intentions, shouting across the vast distance that a few feet can contain: "Uncle Jesse, we brought you a nice mess of butter beans." "What's that? What's that?" And when it had all been restated by his wife—standing tall and gaunt beside him in a flowered dress that reached the ground, her habitual attire, and her hat, the only one we ever saw her wear, an ever-present black straw with red cherries that spilled across the brim and dangled before her eyes as she talked—and understood by him at last, there would be a nodding of acceptance; then, to the wife: "Who is it? Whose boy is it? Emmett's boy? Emmett Cooper's boy?" or, in the case of my mother: "Is it Jennie? Is it Jennie Anderson?" Women were always given their maiden names by Uncle Jesse; gods need not acknowledge such superficial alterations as married names, and in that realm in which his memory still served, they were all maidens still, young girls forever passing to and fro on cool summer lawns.

All eccentrics in books became Cousin Emma Boykin, who painted angels on her ceiling and gave each of them her own face. I never knew her, alas, except through my father's stories, since she fulfilled the prophecy of her painting and joined the heavenly angels long before I was born, but she also wrote a song and I know it; indeed, sing it upon request to skeptical friends. It is called "Mizpah" and the lyrics go:

> I stroll back to the old mill stream
> And there I sit and dream
> Of the promises you made
> In the old magnolia shade

And list to the sad moan
Of a far distant dove
And just dream of your whispers of love.

There is more, of course, but that's enough to prove that it exists,
and very probably I am the only person alive who remembers it.
The rhyme scheme is relentless, true, and so is the beat—her
talents were simple and direct and uncomplicated by great skill,
but the impulse was unquestionably sincere, and it meant a great
deal to me to know that one of my backwoods kin had actually
created works of art (so to speak) and the stream referred to in
the song was still there to be seen and wondered at, ambling
peacefully along beside the ruins of Grandpa's grist mill, with its
collapsed water wheel and its great unmovable stones; all solid and
substantial proof that the familiar stuff of my life could one day,
through the alchemy of art, be made immortal. It gave one something to ponder over.

The beauties in books were my Aunt Jewell. Romantic fellows
were Cousin Maurice, dark and dashing; I always picture him
rushing away on long legs, bent on some mysterious lover's errand.
Big Daddies were Uncle Woodrow; he invented the genre. The
gentleman in Tennessee Williams's play was to me, by comparison, an understated copy. A great bull of a man, incredibly robust
and hearty, Uncle Woodrow strode the earth as if the globe were
his fief and he too large to be contained within its boundaries. The
lion roar of his voice made others' seem pale and timid. He was
the center of attention in any group; he dominated the very air
about him, and I cannot imagine him seated or sleeping or in a
room alone. Adored, respected, even feared, with a suggestion of
danger about him, he was, it seemed to me, forever emerging
triumphant from some scrape or other, bearing on his face a
number of scars as trophies of the wrecks he'd walked away from.
He drove gigantic cars at breakneck speeds, and spectators could

only scramble for safety and marvel at his talent for surviving. Once when I was grown and living in Italy, my mother wrote in a letter, "The man your Uncle Woodrow shot didn't die," and moved on to other family matters as if no more information were called for. I wrote for further facts, and she replied that some unwise person, obviously a stranger in town, had made the mistake of striking Uncle Woodrow's car with his cane.

Fallen women were poor, tragic Myrtle. Every family has a Myrtle and her misfortune we do not discuss.

Fat men were (and are) Charlie McGowan, naturally called "Tiny." Tiny sat on his front porch, rocked, spat tobacco juice onto the ground, and watched the world go by. He was not a relative, but no matter; when families have lived alongside each other for more than a hundred years, it counts for the same thing. If he could be persuaded to dislodge his vast bulk from his long-suffering chair, he could execute an amazingly agile buck and wing and delight his audience with his lyric tenor rendition of "Only a Rose." And, if he could be believed, his romantic conquests in earlier days, across seven counties, would sorely have tried the talents of Casanova. Probably I'm doing an unfortunate disservice to the portly, but to the thin all fat men look alike; certainly I've been meeting Tiny in different disguises all over the world. When I found myself sitting on a couch in Rome next to that swollen and disgraced exile, King Farouk, I knew that behind the dark glasses and the vague aura of former grandeur it was only Tiny, so I talked with His Majesty about the same subjects that would have interested my Mississippi friend—women and food. The sex talk we can skip here, but I told Farouk about the hot dog and hamburger stand at which I had worked in Hollywood, where our specialties were served dripping with chili, onions, and grated cheese, and that high-born gentleman drooled and asked for details just as eagerly as Tiny would have. The circumstances of their birth were hardly similar, but the essentials of their character were the same. King Farouk even commented afterward to some persons from the press that I was the most sophisticated American he had ever met. I do not know with what topics the unsophisticated generally try to engage the interest of a king (genealogy, perhaps, or the treachery of army officers), but it has been my experience that if he's fat and you've worked at a hamburger stand, you can strike him as a pretty extraordinary fellow.

Of course, when you are the sort of person who sees people this way, you assume they understand their own specialness. One thinks that Miss Trotwood will know that she is Miss Trotwood, Micawber will know he's Micawber; they will recognize the thing that drew Dickens to them, that they have a distinctiveness, a uniqueness, that has occurred only once in the world, and it comes as a shock to me that they do not perceive this in themselves and in each other. To me the members of my own family will always be characters of extraordinary depth and color and size, and yet they seem to go about their lives completely unaware of their historic importance. I suppose to the world they seem like average, ordinary people, but it seems incredible to me that this could be so. It would not strike me as unnatural if they, like movie stars, were to be recognized and approached with excitement by strangers on foreign streets.

There is an old Scottish proverb that says, "He whose family has in it neither whore, knave, nor fool was begat by a bolt of lightning." In any case, there are all sorts of persons in families, each has his place in the scheme of things, and I delight in diversity. In my day the casts were large and the roles were many. There was usually the one who played around, the one who always lost his job, the one who gossiped, the one who got rich, the one who got religion, the one who drank, and at least one who was just plain bad. There was, in most households, at least one spinster relation of forgotten degree, who was live-in and unpaid baby-minder, recorder of family history, nourisher of romantic notions, and full-time martyr to a lifelong accumulation of undiagnosed ills. Parents, sisters, brothers, feuding neighbors, and Crazy George—all were members of a larger-than-life stock company, new variants of whom, as long as one was to live, one would cast and recast as one chose the people who played roles in one's life.

The family arena was a battleground on which some skirmishes were lost and some were won; it was a place where rages flared and hatreds blazed, but we cared and we kept track. The family was a community, and once you found your place in it, you were armored for citizenship beyond it in the great Family of Man.

But they tell us now it's all over. New ways are going to be found. The fashion these days is for change, and the rush for change, the race for the new, is so frantic, the pace so accelerated, that the less venturesome among us can get quite dizzy even standing still and looking on. We hear and read daily about startling new breakthroughs, new life forms and styles, new quick cures for sick souls, new "fun" treatments for ailing lives; and nobody asks what happened to yesterday's miracle discovery. It would seem, with all the new announcements, that all our problems should have been solved with last evening's edition of the newspaper. Instead, we look about and see our neighbors standing in shock, exhausted from the running, neck-deep in "How to Discover Your Real Self" books, panic and hunger visible in their eyes, sadly clinging to the hope that tomorrow's pill will make everything right.

It won't, and there's no reason why it should. Our lives are trial and error, joy and sorrow, work and rest, some peace and some turmoil, and our happiness consists of living the good and the bad, of keeping our wits about us, of holding onto a little pluck, of cherishing those things that embellish life and rejecting those things that diminish it. The nirvanas and promises of instant gratification being merchandised these days have about as much substance as the enlightenment of those rich ladies who tell you they went to India for two weeks and found "this marvelous peace" while gazing out the windows of their air-conditioned hotels, presumably past the bodies of the dying babies in the streets.

Individual fulfillment is all the rage now. One's loyalty is only toward one's own self-realization. We read almost daily, sometimes in admiring accounts, of mothers and fathers who, encouraged by their therapists and their envious friends, announce that they are renouncing all prior commitments (made before their consciousness got raised) and are belatedly setting out to find their true roles in the world. Their bewildered and abandoned children are on their own. God knows what is supposed to happen to *their* fulfillment, *their* sense of worth. Where are these children expected to find that sense of identity their newly liberated parents are out beating the bushes for? The mind boggles.

Chaos remains chaos however cheerfully it may be disguised as freedom.

Let us, then, spare a few words in praise of the family before we casually wave it away into extinction, this battered institution that has enabled us to survive all these centuries, and provided the climate, the nourishment, and the soil from which man's greatness has sprung; let us, at least, take a look at what it has been or what, at its best, it has aspired to. Let us reflect upon its failings and its accomplishments; let us examine its past and its possibilities.

3

On the Expertness of the Experts

*"An expert is one who knows more and more about
less and less."* —NICHOLAS MURRAY BUTLER

*"Our wisdom is not less at the mercy of fortune than
our property."* —LA ROCHEFOUCAULD

Generally, books are written by experts. That is as it should be.
We are a practical people, a nation in trade, in a sense, and we
are accustomed to getting fair exchange for our money, so when
we lay out our hard cash for a product, we quite reasonably want
to know that the person who devised it knows more about it than
we do. In the case of a book the judicious buyer should be able
to inspect the jacket and find there the author's credentials, so
that he may wisely judge whether that author is a proper authority
in his field, and ascertain whether his background and training
seem sufficient to justify an investment of time, attention, and
money. That is an entirely sensible expectation. The stores are
crowded with volumes on almost any specialization the human
mind can invent, from sex to the stock market and back again,
with some startling combinations and resourceful overlappings in
between, and the studious public grabs them up as happily as if
they were salvation itself. I do not quarrel with that; fortunes are
being made; capital is being spread around; the readers are being
kept off the streets; doubtless many are helped; and, let us hope,

we'll all soon know everything we always wanted to know about everything.

I am mentioning this early on so that you will be warned: I am not an expert. This does not bother me very much, for I began somewhere along the line to mistrust the expertness of the experts. One has only to witness any random group of them in convocation, arguing among themselves, to feel an awful writhing of terror deep in one's belly. For this they are not to be blamed. They are only doing what their training and experience and their own special insights have led them to do. The trouble is with us. We have placed a childlike trust in specialists of all kinds. The scientists have accomplished wonders in our time and will accomplish more, but this has given us an excess of faith in experts. We've formed fatally unrealistic expectations of them, expectations that lead us into nagging and undefined feelings of having been betrayed. We've come to believe that there should be a handy formula for every problem, and what we've gotten are new names for old diseases. To label a pain is not to cure it, and important-sounding words will work no magic. I do not set down these unfriendly remarks in order to diminish the work or the service to mankind rendered by those heroes who have prolonged our lives, preserved our vitality, and eased our discomforts. I only wish to point out that we still hurt where it matters most, and it hurts more all the time. Each season brings a new crop of prophets, whom we follow in sickening zigzag patterns, and still we howl with an agony of soul. The notion has sometimes dawned on me that one could not be greatly blamed for beginning to suspect that the only expert on the subject of oneself is oneself. At the very least, one can be counted on to keep one's own symptoms straight.

These are, of necessity, personal reflections, for, as should by now be clear, I am neither social scientist, anthropologist, psychiatrist, prophet, nor priest, and their confidence and self-assurance and divine inspiration are not in me. But as God and the mailman know, we have already been inundated with charts and statistics, prescriptions and predictions, to say nothing of pieties and platitudes, from all those learned gentlemen. We have worried over their conclusions, chewed and swallowed and digested them, but in the end we have to go where in the end we always have to go, to the human heart. And it's not all that desperate a thing to do, for, beyond reason and beyond erudition, there exists in us some well of inner quiet, some unexplained source of understanding, that, for want of any better term, we might call a kind of wisdom of the heart. From that well we draw consolation, comprehension, and enlightenment. From it come those flashes of intuition and invention, those leaps of insight, that make our lives into something more than the hunting, eating, and sleeping bodies that we started out as, that make of man a creature who will, as William Faulkner claimed in his Nobel Prize acceptance speech, not only endure but prevail.

The family first happened before any dawn of reason, when men followed impulses more than logic, their hearts more readily than their heads—which were, so far as we know, not yet functioning all that well. It was a creative impulse, as well as a protective drive, a reaching out on the part of male and female to come together to protect and nourish their young. It was there that the notion first arose that a group of people could cling together not only for the satisfaction of physical drives and for mutual protection but to create an entity in which the needs and feelings of others could be recognized and possibly cherished. Family began with the first primitive stirrings of the heart toward generosity, and it seems to have evolved along with us as part of what we are; it was not, as its critics sometimes seem to be saying, an artificial form imposed from the outside. There would appear to be something instinctive about it, since we see the form reflected in one way or another in the lives of our less cerebral feathered or four-footed cousins. Surely among all the devisings of man which have managed thus far to survive, it is high on the list of the most attractive, and chief among those worth saving.

4

Going Home

O dream of joy! is this indeed
The lighthouse top I see?
Is this the hill? is this the kirk?
Is this mine own countree?
—COLERIDGE

My heart's in the Highlands, my heart is not here;
My heart's in the Highlands, a-chasing the deer;
A-chasing the wild deer, and following the roe—
My heart's in the Highlands wherever I go.
—ROBERT BURNS

Thomas Wolfe wrote a book and called it *You Can't Go Home Again.* That is a catchy title and it caught on. It caught on with people, even, who know nothing of the great autobiographical novel that went with it. One often hears it quoted, repeated with the half-jocular, half-embarrassed shrug that accompanies axioms from the Bible, Shakespeare, or *Poor Richard's Almanac.* As is usual with such popular utterances, it caught on precisely because it is part profound truth and part arrant nonsense.

We recognize the truth of it because each of us has at one time or another undertaken that almost mythical journey back to the familiar landscape that used to be home, to confront, instead, a land that is foreign and unfamiliar. That this is so is, of course, not the fault of the place. A place, after all, is only trees, ground, water, soil, and the uses men have put them to. We must credit it, instead, to the heavy burden we lay upon the trip. We go encumbered by an unreasonable demand, unspoken and not even totally formed, that in some mysterious way the questions of a lifetime should be answered there, the hungers of a lifetime assuaged. We hope, perhaps, that we will be able to reach back in time and correct something in our shaping that needs correcting. I dream from time to time that I am making improvements on the house I grew up in, though this house has not existed for ten years. We take with us a troubling sense of longing and of loss. We travel with a haunting mixture of memory and desire. We set out on the nostalgic road with the hope and faith and expectation of the child that once was, with that child's tenderness and innocence, which are not only not what they were but perhaps never even existed as they are recalled, and which are, in fact, an adult's poignant, reconstructed, partly calculated, and carefully nurtured idea of what he himself has been.

He expects to see the giants of his childhood and to know once more those towering and superhuman parents and teachers, neighbors and friends who gave form and shape to his youth, who seemed to move in a world of assurance and competence, and whose eyes were the mirrors in which he first formed images of himself. He expects or hopes to find them not the ordinary mortals they are, with limited knowledge, primitive notions, and narrow interests, complaining about the rising cost of meat and boasting about the town's recent erection of a power plant, but the concerned, judicious, all-knowing authorities he remembers, who once gave him answers and quieted his fears.

He expects to find intact and unchanged the church and the school that helped to mold him, which were so much more than wood and stone and once seemed absolute and everlasting and immovable, guardians of all the certainty in the world, where the depth and breadth of his thoughts, feelings, and impulses were first plumbed.

He finds that they have vanished. If they are physically there, unchanged even, they have become somehow shrunken, diminished, flat, and devoid of any life he recognizes, peopled by strangers of a smaller and lesser race, a company now of dwarfs whose comings and goings have nothing of the burning passions, swelling ambitions, consuming thoughts, raging fears, strange intensities, compelling laughter, or vexing tears that he remembered in them and in himself.

And he expects to come upon himself: to see the towheaded youth, all eager eyes and lengthening bones, with fair freckled skin under a frayed straw hat, barefoot and in overalls, climbing the red clay hill with the distracted air of the born daydreamer, the pale, lonely prince somehow disguised as the farmer's son.

But he is not there. Instead, there are ghosts, glimpses, and hints that tease and tantalize. While he was not looking, life went on. Faces, minds, bodies have altered. The very look of the land has changed. Where once there were hills, there is flat land. It is all gone, washed away by a thousand rains. During the decades it has flowed across the fields, along the ditches, and down the little river, on to bigger rivers, and eventually out to the great uncaring sea. It seems so simple but so unlikely that so much could flow so surely away on such a little stream, that little stream with the Indian name that sits now, hardly moving, evaporating under a hot summer sun.

But so it is, and, instead, he comes upon himself as a middle-aged man with a tiring body, a declining spirit; he is thrown back upon the person he has become.

He sees people. He is hailed by those he knew. He is recognized and remembered. His hand is shaken and his back is slapped, and he in his turn shakes hands and slaps backs. Smiles and hearty remarks are exchanged, but they know nothing of what the years have been for him, little of his dreams for himself or of his place in the world. As he knows nothing of them and of theirs. Together they recall the past; they compare dates and occurrences;

they shake their heads over those who have died or been ruined; they smile with pride over children who have become doctors or salesmen or computer scientists or housewives or mothers, and they joke about the improbable presence of a generation of grand-children. Photographs are displayed. Cheerfully they deny in each other the evidence of graying or vanishing hair and withering flesh. Then they go their separate ways, making promises that will not be kept, wearing a glow that will last for a little, relishing for a time the tender residue of that reaching out, that tentative touching of another familiar life, cherishing the moments of sweet reunion with someone who is not quite a stranger, someone with whom there is something of a shared past, but afterward feeling more lonely, more alone, and more mortal, feeling some-how disturbed, somehow at a loss, somehow less enlightened, and altogether more puzzled about the meaning in it all.

That much, then, of Thomas Wolfe's title is true. But in another sense there is foolishness in it because, as no one knew better than Thomas Wolfe, we go home in our thoughts all the time, sometimes when we have no idea we are doing it. We have in truth never left home, for we carry it around with us. It is a part of our dreaming and our waking. It is a part of our breathing. It is a part of all we have been, all we are, and all we shall ever be. I doubt that there is a day in my life in which some fleeting image of that treasured country does not cross my inner eye. I will suddenly become aware that I have been standing beside the path that led down to the pump behind the schoolhouse, or I will for a moment see clearly the two giant hickory trees beside the road to Grandma's. I will remember the pervading smell of new over-alls on the first day of school or the act of lighting the kerosene lamps in the kitchen and the comforting aroma of the biscuits a busy mother made for our supper. I remember driving the cows home from the pasture in the late afternoons, under the red sky of sunset, moving slowly and lazily, striking with my stick at weeds along the path, dreaming hazy dreams of glory, watching out for snakes and stinging nettles, avoiding the cows' droppings. I can close my eyes and know once more the lurking sense of terror as twilight faded and darkness gathered in clumps at the edge of the woods. I can hear the wail of the congregation singing at night in the church nearby, the collective sound of it floating mournfully through the still mystery of a starlit world, riding on the air with the scent of honeysuckle or crabapple bloom, and mingling in my ear with the cries of crickets, of frogs, of whippoorwills, and the rhythmic creaking of the porch swing I sat in. I recall the novelty of an airplane passing overhead and my sister Janice, who had never seen one on the ground, speaking both our thoughts when she said, "I don't want a plane to fall, but if one is going to fall, I wish it would fall near here so we could see it."

Sometimes walking and talking with my sons, I will hear in my own voice the voice of my father echoing from all those years ago, and I will know once again the strange fascination his mysterious presence held for me. I hear his rich voice vibrate against the trees we move among, and in it I can now hear something of pain, something lost and lonely, I was then too young to recognize or suspect in others.

I remember the sights and sounds and smells of home because the memory of home is the thing that never leaves us.

There is a familiar old saying, "You can take the boy out of the country but you can't take the country out of the boy," and, whatever your country has been, however alien it may have seemed to you at the time, or however alien to it you may have felt, it is forever a part of what you are, what you become, and what you mourn for.

And the core of it, the center around which all revolves, is the family: the father that was, the mother that was, the brothers and sisters, the uncles, aunts, grandparents, friends and neighbors— all exist forever in some part of what you are and what you do.

They are as inescapable as life, as inevitable as death, and even if you somehow shut them out of your waking mind, they remain a part of everything that moves, molds, and renews you. You live with them and they with you.

5

Of Fathers and Mothers

"Mother is the name for God in the lips and hearts of little children." —W. M. THACKERAY

"The fathers have eaten sour grapes, and the children's teeth are set on edge." —Ezekiel 18:2

It has been a cliché of my generation to complain of the emotional problems with which we were saddled by those insensitive and unworthy creatures who happened, by some unexplained mishap, to have become our parents. When I was in college, the talk in the coffee shops, once Gide and Rilke and Hemingway and Fitzgerald had been pigeonholed, categorized, and nicely disposed of, was likely to linger long on a recitation of all the awful things those parents had done to us that had turned us into the fascinating creatures we were. It was a source of considerable pride, and we were not above boasting about the complexes they had unwittingly inflicted upon us. We spent many a delightful hour piling up indictments against our elders. We had read our Freud, or, more accurately, we had read *about* Freud, and, though our understanding may have been slight, we had picked up enough to clasp him to our hearts. Our infatuation with the trappings of psychology was shameless; we could and did sprinkle into our conversations, with the same careless abandon with which we sprinkled salt onto our hamburgers, all the popular

32

terms like "inferiority complex," "trauma," "penis envy" (all the girls claimed that one in those days; I believe it's been falling into disfavor of late), "Oedipal yearnings" (very big), "suppression" and "repression"—these last two being particular bugbears, we would never admit that they applied to us. They were applied most often to previous generations; we ourselves tried to appear liberated and vastly experienced in sensual matters, not a pose easily maintained by nervous near-virgins. Indeed, we were sometimes inspired to exaggerate the extent of our wounds, the depravity of our home lives. It added a needed touch of glamour. Not to have had a miserable childhood was a badge of disgrace, a certain sign of lack of sensitivity. It would have been a hardy soul who would have dared confess to such a thing. To have emerged from a happy home was too middle-class a phenomenon to be admitted; there was no artistry in it. Arguments broke out over whose childhood had been the worst, and more than one of us, ambitious for social acceptance, was suspected of inventing a case of incest to lend our background a bit of color.

Our intellectualism had more than a little desperation in it. We had grown up in the era of the Andy Hardy series and other films that glorified a certain kind of innocence in American life and we now felt compelled to reject it. Those films were never quite true, of course, and probably we had never entirely believed in them at the time; yet they had enough of truth that for a while we did convince ourselves that we were like that.

We were right when we said that family life, in America or elsewhere, had never been quite as warm, wholesome, uncomplicated, and attractive as it was in the film *Meet Me in St. Louis*, for instance, and we were rebelling against the hypocrisy and self-congratulation we saw in it. Booth Tarkington, whose sunny comedies had delighted an earlier generation, we dismissed as a total fraud and beneath our contempt. Even Thornton Wilder, whose intellect, craft, and originality we could not ignore, we viewed with some alarm. He was sentimental, we said, as dirty a word as existed in our language. I had wept when I first read *Our Town* and I can weep when I read it today, but for that period of my life I had learned to suppress tears. Tears were for the weak and the simple-minded, while life was harsh and cruel and had to be looked at with unblinking directness. It would, in fact, be some years before I would again permit myself the pleasure of weeping, and then I had to relearn the art. Now, in contrast, I have in my riper years become rather like Mr. Raspberry and weep easily; even, I'm afraid, rather often. Just recently I took my children to see a movie called *Conrack*, a touching film about an idealistic and energetic young man, full of a lusty appetite for life, trying to reach some impoverished children in an isolated community; to give them some glimpse of beauty, he put a record on the phonograph and out came Brahms's "Lullaby." My kids got very excited. "Daddy, it's your song," they both said in astonishment. It took me a moment to realize what they meant. Every night since they were babies I have sat in their room singing them to sleep with Brahms's "Lullaby," and they had thought it was a tune I'd made up. I had been singing it for so long that I, too, had long since forgotten that it had a name and a composer. It is surprising, really, that they connected my unmusical croaking with the piece itself, beautifully played by an orchestra in the film. Anyway, without their knowing it, I sat there for a long time with tears rolling down my face, weeping not out of sadness, except in some roundabout way that had to do with time passing, and with the elusiveness of moments, but mostly for the miracle of them, the boys, for the miracle of their minds, their excitement, their buoyancy, their beauty, their love. I wept for the joy of them.

But back in my college days we had banished from our lists of what was allowed not only sentimentality but sentiment as well.

Eugene O'Neill was our spokesman. His towering gloom and brutal passion, his powerful tragedies of guilt and suffering and hatred and vengeance, his sagas of families in which the various members tore at each other, wounding, torturing, devouring, and destroying each other—those fitted our view of the world. We liked Sherwood Anderson, too, with his small-town people living lives of quiet desperation, his suppressed women running screaming and naked into a Middle Western night; that seemed more like the norm to us.

And August Strindberg. We discovered him in college. His work seethes with rage, obsessions, insanity, hatred of women, and despair at life. Others may have talked of him as a special talent, extraordinary and singular in the history of literature, but we spoke of him as if he were a detached and realistic observer, and of his work as if it were recognizable and accurate reporting on the pitfalls of family life as we ourselves had experienced it. To hear us talk, you would have thought that where we grew up Tennessee Williams's characters were the kids next door. (Which, come to think of it, some of them were.)

Well, so much for that. If there is anything one learns as one gets older, it is that completely opposite points of view can both be totally and equally true. Strindberg was right, but so—barring any consideration of literary merit—was Louisa May Alcott. O'Neill told the truth, and so did Thornton Wilder.

And our judgments were not really literary judgments at all, and had little to do with any evaluations of those works we might make at any later time. Our opinions grew, instead, out of our own needs at that period in our lives; they were colored by the stages of our personal development, and determined finally by our insecure groping toward some kind of certainty about ourselves. Our attitude toward our families, and toward that literature that portrayed families, was in some part an expression of our normal and necessary rebellion against our dependency upon those families. We were trying to work up the courage to be on our own, and to do so, we had to, I suppose, renounce those emotional ties that were so very binding, and denounce the views they represented as well. It seems to be the common experience in the lives of the young that a time comes when they look at their parents with scorn, finding them foolish, uninformed, misguided (to put it civilly), and (this hurts) unprincipled. Their allegiance is to their own peers; they have to affect an independence of mind that they do not yet feel; and they are able, by clinging together, to reassure and reinforce one another. It is astonishing to read literature from centuries past and find in it the same complaints about the young and about changing times, to find that at every stage of history it was said that the young were going to the dogs, that all the real values were being swept away, and that the end of the world could be expected at any moment.

We were rejecting in order to form our own values. That was part of it. The other part was that we were in a different generation and there were truly deep and sharp departures from the previous generations. (They've become increasingly sharper with each successive generation since.) Values *had* changed. We *did* have to take the new psychological findings into our consideration. Freud had given us a new interpretation of behavior, and we had to use it. We were by and large more educated, if less shaped by experience, less touched by mature responsibilities, than our parents had been at our ages, and if we were self-conscious about it, pompous, humorless, smug, and overbearing in our protestations of our virtues and our proclamations of our idealism, then we were only doing what new generations probably have the right to do.

And there was then already the beginning of special problems that have since become even more pronounced: what we had learned at home had not always prepared us to take our places in an uncertain world; there was less of a sense of purpose, or perhaps I simply mean that we were under less pressure to start earning our own livings. There had begun that blurring of sex roles that has grown steadily since then, a lack of certainty about what was expected of persons of each gender. With our larger degree of self-awareness, and living as we did under less severe social pressures and community guidelines, we had to feel our way into new kinds of relationships. More than any previous generation, we were to determine our own paths, to shape our own destinies. Certainly this was true for those who, like myself, had emerged from farm communities where life had not changed significantly for generations. It was a long step from Quitman to Berkeley, California, and I was not the only one at the university there who had made such a leap. Few intended to return to their home towns and live out their lives in patterns similar to those of their parents; there were more choices open to us, and the prospect of unbounded freedom was frightening. In our shows of new-found sophistication we were bravely whistling in the dark.

Too, we were not lying when we said we had been scarred by our parents' psychological problems, though it was not new for parents to have problems and it was not new that their children should be scarred by them. What was new was our perception of our wounds and our manner of dealing with them, when an earlier generation would simply have denied or ignored them. That we chose, in our confusion and anxiety, to dramatize them for our own glorification was at least a beginning. When we are young, it is hard to recognize or accept that parents' problems are problems; we see everything in our own terms, that is, how it relates to us, and parents are not allowed to have problems unto themselves. From our point of view, parents exist, after all, for us, and it is only when we are older looking back that we can see those things in them that disturbed us as difficulties no less painful to them than to us; only then, from the perspective of our experience with our own weaknesses, can we recognize as pain for them what we took to be perversity directed toward us.

I talked with my friends, at length and late into the nights, chiefly about my conflicts with my father, which were, God knows, real enough, but even in the telling I invented a somewhat more glamorous character than I truly believed him to be. I would relate (not without pleasure) how he would leave me waiting outside various neighbors' houses while he went inside to cohabitate with the wives—a dash of sex, and one's early exposure to same, gave a bit of glitter to one's image in those innocent days. I told about a time when we were riding along a street in Quitman in the buggy. We passed a house where a lady was watering the flowers in her front yard. He stopped the buggy. "How do?" he said. "How do?" she answered. There was a pause. Her watering can, suspended halfway toward a bunch of petunias, did not move. "I know something better to be doing," he said. "Come in and have a cup of coffee," she said. He handed the reins to me and climbed down. Half an hour later he was back and we took off with Papa singing a bawdy song, something about "Old Aunt Molly, God bless her, threw her leg over the dresser. . . ."

I would repeat the advice he gave me. ("Take a leak as soon as you finish and always wash it off with soap and water," or: "You have a day gal and a night gal. The day gals are the ones you marry. The night gals are for night purposes.") That was always good for a big laugh from my audience. I told those stories well, and I built him up as a charming rogue, but I did not ever really talk about the outrage and shame I felt at the time—my emphasis was upon the stimulation. The truth was too painful and the good storyteller learns how to turn his pain into humor. Nor did I tell, because I'd long since stopped bothering to remember what I really liked about him, how he used to take me with him when I was little more than a toddler, on hunting trips, or into town for the day, or while he went about his work on the farm. He would saddle up the horse and say, "Run into the house and tell your mother you're going with me over to Uncle John's." Often my mother would protest, but I would already be climbing up to sit wedged in front of him in the saddle. He talked to me about everything and anything that came into his mind, however unsuitable it may sometimes have been, treating me as a reasoning, reasonable human being. Never mind the fact that I was soon disagreeing and disapproving of practically everything he said; the point is that he regarded me as a thinking person, and because he did, I so regarded myself.

He instilled in me, without my knowing it, something of his passion for the land, his kinship with nature. My earliest and most pleasant memories of him are connected with nature: standing close to him in the darkness of night when all was clear and silent and still, and gazing up, up, past countless miles into the endless expanse of stars over us, while he pointed out the Little Dipper, the Big Dipper, and the mysterious North Star that was always north, and, because it was, you could never be lost no matter where you were, for as long as you knew how to find it, you knew where north was. Or at daybreak pausing, as he paused, in the front yard and peering, as he peered, at those first streaks of light across the sky that told you, if you knew how to read the signs, what kind of day was promised. Or moving with him in the soft, sweet haze of early morning through fields of dew-covered grass, and feeling all life beginning to stir around us. Or sitting beside him in the door of the barn while he smoked and we watched the rain falling outside, collecting in puddles and forming little rivulets that ran across the lot.

He had more than a little madness in his makeup; he was possessed by a wild vision of life and a seething discontent plagued him into prolonged and terrifying fits of rage, yet certainly we, his children, knew and took for granted that the major drive of his life was for his family and that all that was left of his hopes and expectations was tied up in us.

In all cultures there is a role for the woman and another for the man in the rearing of children. There have been those in which responsibility for the child was invested in the mother's father or brother rather than in the biological father, others in which the mother looks after the child so long as it is physically dependent upon her for survival, after which the father assumes sole responsibility; but always there is some arrangement made in which both sexes participate in the care and instruction of the child. The things that are taught may vary, but the purpose remains basically the same. The function of the family has always been to bear children, to provide for them, and to prepare them to take care of themselves and to fill a role in the community. In the past, when there had been a question of the survival of the group or tribe, there was a great deal of emphasis on the importance of the child to the community, and the whole clan might take an interest in his survival and in his training. It is only in comparatively recent times that men and women have married for no purpose other than their own happiness, having nothing to do with the welfare of their group or the future of the race. Marriage then became a private and individual matter, not a function of the community, and as this situation has grown to be the prevailing one, responsibility for the care of children has come to rest almost totally within the family unit.

Within the protection of that unit, the child learns what form of behavior is acceptable and what is not. He learns that there are differences between being a boy and being a girl, and he learns the different tasks that are assigned to each and which are shared. He learns attitudes toward family members, toward those outside the home, toward religion, toward growing up, toward death. He compares his father, his mother, his home, to others in his world and he forms judgments about them. He learns to cope with brothers and sisters, how to relate to other persons who enter the home.

Today, as our civilization has grown more complex, traditional roles have become less defined, and the outlines have become blurred and no longer have the same meaning, but at my time in Pleasant Grove things were still laid out pretty much as they had been in my grandparents' time. Women bore babies, took care of them, cooked, looked after the house, and, when they could, worked in the fields, hoeing or picking cotton. Sometimes they milked the cows, though in some houses that was men's work, or it might be assigned to one of the older children. The women almost always looked after the chickens, feeding them, gathering the eggs, arranging the nests for sitting hens. Religion was often the woman's province; she was expected to take the children to church, though there were some houses, unlike mine, in which the father played an active part in church matters.

Men might play with babies but did not bathe or feed them. They worked outside in the fields, did carpentry repairs, all the heavy work, but rarely cooking or other housekeeping tasks. They hunted, fished, smoked cigarettes, sometimes drank, and were most of them pretty adept at cussing.

Girls learned from their mothers how to cook and sew, and boys, as soon as they could tumble after them, followed their fathers into the field, taking pride in the little tasks they were allowed to do. I can remember little boys of three or four strutting about in barn lots, pushing cows into stalls and yelling at the horses, assuming their father's stance and, by the time they entered school, talking with assurance of crops and harvests, boasting about how much they could do.

All in all, and for the most part, it worked quite well in its time. Women were thought to be sensitive, gentle, emotional, and weak of will. Men were hard-muscled, tough, and without fear. They never cried, no matter what happened. As a boy or girl you discovered where you fitted in, and it was fairly easy to fall into the pattern; if you didn't quite fit, you bluffed your way through the best way you could, and certain allowances were made.

Sometimes, though, it was not quite that simple. It was not for me, and I realize now that one reason for this was that it had never been quite that simple for my father, though I did not realize it then.

He was a strange man, complex and contradictory, and when I think of him now, when I picture his face or when I start to describe him, the person I think of is very different from the figure I thought I knew when he was alive. I saw him then as a towering figure of potency and power, threat and menace, and I lived in fear of and in resistance to all that I held him to be. Recently I was given a photograph of him taken when he was seventeen. I look at that face, and, incredibly, it is the same face I was to meet for the first time twenty-three years afterward: sad and removed, anticipating rejection, with dark wounded eyes turned inward toward remembered pain. The pose is tentative and unsure, and suddenly I remember his movements, which were, in some moments, unbearably uncertain. There is no hint in the photograph of the gaiety and high spirits of which he was capable, or of the animal grace with which he sometimes carried himself, or of the charm and magnetism with which he could, in an expansive mood, completely captivate the unwary; there is no indication of his delight in narrative or the pleasure with which he held his audiences. In the picture there is only the apprehensive look, as if he might at any moment take flight, and the hooded, suffering eyes, and I wonder how in all those years with him I failed to see it.

Actually, there is no mystery, and I did not fail to see it. The truth is that there was only one step from the woeful eyes to the look of madness that I recall. When the volcano of anger and frustration erupted inside him, these same eyes burned with rage and destruction and he struck out wildly and blindly; accusations, curses, ranting insanities poured from him in a sustained explosion directed at my mother, at his absent father, at her absent mother, or at the heavens or at the absurdity of existence; an ongoing outburst that seemed somehow as madly logical and as senselessly rational as Lear on the moor shouting into the thunder.

I now know why he was not physical in these outbursts—he never struck either her or us; the punishment was only verbal, the cruel and compulsive lashing of a venomous tongue. And the punishment, I now understand, was directed at himself.

Once when he was five or so, Carter, with his strange intuitions, asked me suddenly and without preamble, "Did you like your father very much?" I was startled, but I told the truth. "No," I said, "I didn't," and I told him why. Mostly it was that he made me feel so badly about myself. He used to yell at me when I performed ineptly, as I invariably did, at rugged tasks. I remember vividly an occasion when I was hardly tall enough to reach the handles of the plow I was trying to guide through the wet ground of a cane patch. The wet earth makes the plow go deep and it is hard to control. Certainly my strength was not sufficient, and as it wobbled back and forth, he stood at the end of the row yelling, "You'll never do it. You're no damn good." Carter, in telling the story to his mother later, added an observation of his own, "And naturally, that made Daddy do it that much worse." He had gotten the point, all right. It certainly did, and it is strange that my father could not have noticed that result. He seemed to me to be a bully and a tyrant, and he had no idea of the effect this had on me.

In 1944 we were living in New Orleans, a mysterious foreign city with which I'd begun a lifelong love affair, and where I first discovered such exotic delights as the opera and the ballet. I was seventeen and just out of high school when my father lay down on the sofa in the living room and died. Suddenly I was in charge, the head of the family, a position that I knew perfectly well that I had long wanted to hold, and I set about the execution of immediate duties with calm and assurance. Riding the St. Claude streetcar, I had often noticed a white-columned funeral home called Lammano, Panno and Fallo, so I looked them up in the telephone book and called them. My mother and younger brothers and sisters packed to go to Quitman, where he would be buried at Pleasant Grove. I would leave on a later train with my father's body. I went to the funeral home and picked out the coffin, suit, and tie, and made all the transportation arrangements. I then made whatever telephone calls to Mississippi and elsewhere were necessary, saw that my mother and the children got off, and went back to see the results of Lammano, Panno and Fallo's cosmetic art. They were waiting for my approval, and, with that professional undertaker manner that is, I suppose, the same the world over, that odd blending of unctuousness, a quick and practiced pose of sympathy, and an almost boastful pride in a job well done, all eagerness and full of the expectation of praise, they led me into the room where Papa was laid out under the outstretched arms of a large plaster statue of the Madonna.

I don't know how they had done it, but they'd turned him into an Italian. He looked exactly like an Italian banker. It wasn't just that I was unaccustomed to seeing him dressed up; it wasn't just the black suit and dark tie; there was something excessively combed and waxy in his appearance, almost as if they'd stuck on a little black mustache. He looked uncomfortable and impatient, as I suppose he would in such foreign surroundings—stained-glass windows, gray plush draperies, and religious pictures were hardly his element; he was more truly at home, after all, in the woods in his battered old hunting coat with his dog and his gun—and he looked unfamiliar, but then the dead always look unfamiliar, as if they were a distant relative of the deceased, but a relative with certain strong resemblances. And, of course, there is that terrible stillness of the dead, that almost suggests an affront, a deliberate removal, as if the deceased had somehow chosen so to remove himself, without apology, without regret, and with no consideration for the feelings of those abandoned.

Clutched in his hands was a silver crucifix, an incongruity so astounding that I might have laughed if I had not had a watchful audience in the Messrs. Lammano, Panno and Fallo, who were responsible for the comic outrage. I could imagine the shock with which the sight of that crucifix would have been received when the coffin was opened back in Clarke County. I told them that it should be removed and the men shook their heads in sympathy. "Was Daddy not a Catholic?" one asked gravely, and I responded in the negative with equal gravity, then for a moment I wept. Only for a moment, and not out of grief, but at the absurdity of it all. I did not call him "Daddy," and the use of the term seemed somehow sissy and citified in connection with him. No, he wasn't Catholic. I'm not sure he was even Baptist. He wasn't an un-believer either, exactly. It's just that in his mind God and an afterlife had nothing to do with him. "The Almighty knows about the people up at the church," I've heard him say. "He doesn't know anything about me. When I die, I'll be no different from an old rotten limb falling off a tree and laying on the ground." I was dismayed by the men's moves to comfort me, and my tears withdrew in embarrassment, departing as quickly as they had come. The men removed the offending crucifix and bowed them-selves out of the room, and I was left alone with my father for the last time, and, in a sense, for the first time. I was aware that a change had taken place, that I was now in charge of him and that from now on I was in charge of myself, answerable to myself and responsible to myself.

It was too late for grief; I'd felt grief for him in the past, when he was alive, grief for the awkward, accusing, wounded silences between us, grief for what had long since been lost or rejected or perhaps had never been, grief for a seventeen-year misunderstand-ing that was probably inevitable but which had injured him and had injured me, without either of us understanding that we had the power so to diminish the other. I would later understand that he feared me as much as I feared him, but I did not understand that then.

I understood something else, though. I knew the hollowness of victories. I had won. I was alive, and I would grow in power and strength, but I would never get to know him, never be reconciled with him, never cut through that painful antagonism that hung like a tangible presence in the space between us, never meet him as an equal, never speak to him or with him or even of him without discomfort. I would never understand what moved him. I would never think of him with ease.

In that I was wrong, but a seventeen-year-old could not know that, any more than he could understand that he himself had contributed to and participated in the rejection, had been responsible for his share of it. When you are young, you feel totally without power—or perhaps what you feel is fear for your awakening sense of power: power is something that others have exercised toward you, and that not always in a benign way, so it is something to be feared, even denied, in yourself. When you are groping with the many apparently different persons who seem to exist all at one time inside you, you are not likely to know that the death of your protagonist does not close the book on the relationship, that the manner of your dealing with it will help to determine the kind of man you will become, and that the relationship will, indeed, continue to grow and change as you grow and change, that you will look at it and understand it even as you learn to look at and understand yourself, that you will come to terms with him as you come to terms with yourself.

The young are intolerant and unforgiving toward others and toward themselves, and they have not yet begun that process of self-forgiveness, the acceptance of their own humanness, that makes them recognize and accept the humanness of others.

The young feel obliged to exhibit to the world a composed and finished mask that conceals the chaos and confusion raging underneath, to be, at all costs, a poised and completed figure. The maintenance of such a mask requires a singleness of focus, a denial of that which distracts, and a putting aside of all those perplexing complexities and compounded contradictions that are warring within.

A seventeen-year-old does not know that there are second chances, then third, then fourth. He is too caught up in the drama of himself to understand it. I was, all that day, watching my performance with that other eye with which the self-absorbed observe and take notes on themselves, so that, that evening when the conductor on the train looked at me gravely and asked, "Are you the boy that . . ." leaving the rest of the sentence unfinished, I nodded solemnly, in keeping with the image of myself as a brave youth, forlorn and alone on the Lincoln funeral train making its melancholy way across the darkening miles. The conductor, thinking of the passing of fathers and of his own mortality, asked, "How old?" and I, thinking of myself, answered, "Seventeen."

In between, after all the tasks had been done, the coffin closed, and the phone calls made, there was a stretch of three hours until the departure of the train, so I did what I always do if I have three hours between crises. I went to the movies. I saw *Molly and Me*, and the stars were Gracie Fields and Monty Woolley.

In the years that followed I would sometimes dream that my father came out of his grave and I would tell him that he had to stay there. I do not remember these dreams as having been frightening, and I do not remember my feelings toward him in them as having been particularly unfriendly. They served the function, I think, of reasserting my independence. As time went on, they were spaced further and further apart, and the ease and degree of intimacy with which I encountered him seemed to parallel my unfolding comprehension and acceptance of my own nature.

From his father a son learns what a man does and what it is to be a man. A father, by example and by instruction, prepares his son to take a place in the world. Historically that has meant teaching him to hunt, fight if need be, play, work, make friends, form a family, and to provide for and protect the family. Historically the patterns were set by the culture, and within a particular group, or class, they varied little. In our time, with its prevalence of individually independent families, the success or failure of a particular father-and-son relationship rests largely upon the abilities and maturity of that father. If the father has never resolved his feelings about his own father, has never come to be certain about the meaning of his own manhood, then he is not likely to be the best guide for his son.

Gradually the historically masculine skills, requiring strength, muscle, and physical endurance, have diminished considerably in importance, and parental teaching is at present not very concentrated upon them. Mental processes have become the important ones—attitudes, beliefs, awareness, the ability to evaluate, to think clearly, to communicate with one's fellow men, to accept others, to accept yourself, to love, to be able to express that love, to have self-respect, to extend yourself outwardly into the world, to invest in that world, and in those persons in it, something of the same value and regard that you hold for yourself. Considering that, we can pretty much rewrite the first sentence of the previous paragraph to read: from his father a son learns what a human being does and what it means to be a human being.

In recent years women have been rediscovering themselves in the light of present-day realities, re-examining their traditional roles, and opening up new possibilities for themselves. For men, the adjustment that women are making has had certain beneficial effects, among them a new relaxation about their own gentler and more loving qualities; men have found a new freedom about expressing their emotions, and they feel more rather than less manly in doing so. But when I was young, the masculine world was supposed to be what we now call macho; we were judged and we judged ourselves according to that standard. For a long time it bothered me that I didn't feel quite as fierce and self-sufficient as John Wayne. I don't think it would have bothered me so much if I hadn't thought it bothered other people, if I hadn't thought that the other fellows *did* feel like John Wayne. As I grew up and got to know the other fellows better, I gradually made a discovery. They didn't feel much like John Wayne either. For all I know, nobody feels like John Wayne. If I live long enough, I may find out that John Wayne doesn't feel like John Wayne.

My father didn't feel like John Wayne, but he didn't know that you don't have to; he didn't even suspect that it's all right to admit it to yourself in the privacy of your own mind. The virtues of rugged strength and aggressiveness were requirements in the world he was brought up in, and a part of his torment was that he never judged himself to be adequately equipped in these departments.

He always spoke with tenderness of his mother. It is from one's mother that one first gets a sense of one's worth. The warm softness of her body, the protective support of her arms, the sustenance that comes from her breast, her care, her tenderness, her continuous presence, the soft, soothing sound of her voice, her response to one's outcries, are the first awarenesses one has, and from these things come one's first feelings of being wanted, valued, and treasured. In the beginning years it is the mother who warms, comforts, teaches, and protects, and the child associates tenderness and loving with her. From his mother my father got his sensitivity and his tenderness, neither of which he was ever to feel comfortable about or know quite what to do with.

She was a gentlewoman of some refinement and breeding. Her family had come from Virginia, and they were, I believe, poor relations of the Wyatts who were among the first families to settle in the Virginia Colony, with roots that went far back in English history. She had wanted to call him by her family name, but my grandfather did the naming and he called him Emmett, and my father was thinking of her when he gave me the name she'd intended for him. She died when he was twelve. She put her arms around him, and, referring to my Aunt Cola (short for Pensacola), who was then an infant, she said, "Take care of my baby," and then she died. When he told me about it thirty-five years later, there was a sadness in his voice, the sadness of loss remembered.

He was the third child and the second son in a family of thirteen children. He never spoke of his older brother with anything like affection, and he never spoke of his father in any tone that suggested warm personal feelings, only smoldering resentment, enormous respect, regretful admiration, and a deep-seated (but desperately fought-against) sense of his own failure to measure up to Grandpa's stature.

His father was an overwhelming figure, an extraordinary personality, powerful and commanding even in old age, when I knew him. His name was William Preston Cooper, and he was rich (in terms of that time and place), influential, and well known in east Mississippi and west Alabama. "Prominent Choctaw County Planter and Merchant Dies," *The Meridian Star* said in reporting his death. We were all in awe of him. Tall, proud of bearing, imperious of manner, with an impressive head of white hair and a full pepper-and-salt mustache, he was an unassailable presence, and when he appeared, his grandchildren stopped whatever we were doing—games were abruptly broken off, frivolity abandoned —and stood more or less at attention, all concentration focused on him. It was not that he demanded it—such people don't have to—he simply expected it, took it for granted, and it just happened; and not only with us. I remember once being with my father in Kirkland's Store in Quitman when my grandfather entered. We stood unnoticed to one side while Grandpa made his progress through the store. Hats were removed and respectful greetings offered. "How are you, Uncle Press?" "Mighty good to see you, Captain." And clerks rushed forward to serve him. He accepted the deference as his due, not even noticing that it was deference. His arrogance was so habitual that it seemed like good manners—I never saw him behave toward anybody as an equal—and came off as a gracious sort of condescension. My father watched with a stiff coldness, and when Grandpa moved behind a counter, as if he owned the store, to inspect some merchandise, I said, "I thought you weren't supposed to go behind the counter," and Papa, without removing his eyes from the old man, said in a low, muffled voice, almost as if speaking to himself, "You're not." "But Grandpa did," I insisted. "He ought not to," my father said, and the bitterness and defeat in his voice I can hear now, forty years later.

Grandpa dressed every day as if it were Sunday, and he was partial to white linen suits for winter as well as summer; with them he wore a spotless white Stetson hat. To judge a man, he used to say, you look at his hat and his shoes. My father, in his turn, used to get himself such a Stetson in a sudden burst of confidence. He would look at it, turning it this way and that, and finally, with some pride, put it on, but he never really brought it off, and soon it would be put away to gather dust.

My grandfather owned a store, a grist mill, and twelve hundred acres of land, much of it in virgin timber. He liked to ride about his land on his beloved gray mare, called "Old Mag," and the tenants stopped their work and bowed respectfully as he passed by. This description of him, I know, rather misleadingly calls up an image of the sainted Robert E. Lee, when he actually bore a strong resemblance to Mark Twain, a somewhat different brand of fellow, and if I tell you that some of these tenants knew very well that they sheltered under their roofs children bearing their names but fathered by my grandfather (for he quite openly exercised the practice of *droit du seigneur*), it should banish forthwith any association with the celebrated General Lee.

A number of his illegitimate offspring were almost but not quite openly acknowledged. Of the three I had knowledge of, one had a particularly favored status. I am told that when he was a boy, Rube (as we shall call him, for that was not his name) used to stay with Grandpa for long periods of time and he was accepted by the other children. He even came to Grandpa's funeral, attending with his red-haired mother, by then in her late sixties, who broke down at the cemetery and had to be restrained by her son and his sister when she tried to throw herself onto the grave. They did, though, have the grace to sit on the opposite side of the aisle from us. I don't know that there was ever much attempt at denial of any of this on the part of my grandfather and the family— which was not the way it was in my time about the rumor that my father had an illegitimate daughter. A birth had occurred, a couple had separated, and the accusation had been made; but my father never mentioned it and his sisters and my mother always said it was not true. I do not know, but one of my sisters says that once, in a crowd, she came face to face for a few moments with a girl who was the mirror image of herself.

Even if Grandpa's family had tried to deny it, the effort would have been wasted, because the physical resemblance of all his children to him, on whichever side of the blanket they had been begotten, was unmistakable. Once in town I saw a woman I took to be one of my aunts and I went over and said "Hello." "You must be Emmett Cooper's boy," she said and then she told me she was not my aunt. When I described the episode to my mother, she knew immediately whom I'd spoken to and she was annoyed with me. (Her side of the family was much better behaved.) "I wish you wouldn't go up and speak to strangers," she said. "Just because they look like you doesn't mean they're kin to you."

When Aunt Cola and Aunt Eddie, two of my father's favorite sisters, visited us, they always inquired after Rube, and he would reply, "Saw Rube the other day. Looks more like Pa every day, got that prissy walk of his."

Years later I went with my mother and those two sisters to a reunion of the Wyatt family. My relationship here is a little complicated. (In the days before Henry Ford changed our travel habits, much crisscrossing of kin was inevitable, for the young did not venture far from home to wed.) My Uncle Woodrow, whom I have already described, was a Wyatt and he was married to my mother's sister. He was also my father's first cousin. That's easy enough to grasp, but what follows may be more complicated. One of the ladies who had children by my grandfather was the niece of my grandmother, so her children were Wyatts and related to us as Wyatts, quite apart from their illegitimate relationship through Grandpa. One of those children was at the reunion, which as a Wyatt she had every right to be. My aunts had always known of her, of course, and had often seen her here and there when they were young; but they had always refused to speak to her. If they had not dared cross Grandpa, they could at least snub the half-sister he had given them—one has to take a moral stand somewhere. By now, however, they were all getting old. Grandpa was many years in his grave. They looked alike, unmistakably sisters, and Bessie, she with the bar sinister in her scutcheon, seemed to be an agreeable enough person, obviously prosperous (she was, it turned out, the proprietress of a bar in Memphis, Tennessee), so the three sat down to chat. I was astonished to see that they all shared a characteristic very common in my family: not just the fact that they all talked at the same time—all Wyatts do that, true; they never shut up—but Bessie actually had an identical mannerism that suggests something or other about the influence of heredity over environment. As she talked she punched each listener on the forearm with her index finger. She would punch one and then the other, and they, neither of them realizing it, were punching back with the same gesture. It gives one pause. Passing on the shape of one's nose through a temporary encounter seems simple enough to understand, but the transmission of personal gestures, I should have thought, would require a continuing relationship. I called my mother's attention to Bessie's arm punching, and she looked at it with disinterest. "Just like your granddaddy," she said and moved on to other guests.

When Grandpa was on his deathbed at eighty-three or -four, a couple of his devoted daughters, fearful for his reception in the afterlife, uncharacteristically decided to brave his wrath and get him baptized. That rite, with Baptists, is no simple and delicate sprinkling of water upon the repentant head. If they had only been Methodists, they might have accomplished their purpose while the old man was asleep, but for Baptists only immersion will do; the person of the sinner must be totally submerged in the water, and Grandpa, God knew, had a heavy load of sins to wash away. Furthermore, for the act to have validity, the subject must be fully conscious during its performance. So a bathtub was determined upon as the only suitable and available receptacle, and a local clergyman was called in, chosen not only because he was a family friend and could be counted on for a certain amount of discretion but also because he was as muscular as he was dedicated and both attributes would be essential for the task at hand. The obliging minister, several of the daughters, a son-in-law or two, and a couple of hired hands, all struggled valiantly to do God's work and get Grandpa into the tub, but, dying or not, he fought back fiercely, bestowing upon them all for their efforts, along with some splendid bruises, a shattering outpouring of invectives and curses from his vast storehouse of blasphemies. They had finally to admit defeat, abandon him to the mercy of the Almighty, and allow him to depart the world as unrepentant as he had entered it. Among the other things he shouted to the grieving assembly was that if they'd bring a woman to his bed, he'd have no need of dying.

In a man like my grandfather there is much that delights and excites, much that compels admiration. His children were proud to be his children and to partake of his glamour, just as his second wife, my father's stepmother, was proud to be his wife, though I doubt that he ever appeared in public with her. Soon after the death of my grandmother, he went away somewhere and came back with her sitting modestly in the buggy; he installed her in the house, where she cooked and waited on him and bore him children, but she rarely set foot off the place, just as she rarely spoke when he entertained his visitors. Drab, gray, sweet, and self-effacing, she sat in another room with lesser womenfolk unless called upon for some service. She had, I suppose, been sufficiently honored in the match that it would not occur to her that further rewards or pleasures or display was due her. Always afterward his children would speak of him as one speaks of the exalted, in the hushed and hallowed tones reserved for deities, and they would seem to forget that he somehow diminished them in their own eyes. His specialness captured and held their attention and fired their imaginations, and their sense of their importance was derived from it; at the same time, unless such a man has more sensitivity toward his children than Grandpa Cooper did, their lives are lessened by him. In the case of his daughters the pallid men they would marry would seem tame and uninspired in comparison; in the case of the sons their own lives—no matter how well they might do in the eyes of others—would remain unworthy in their own view, for they would look at themselves from their father's perspective, and a man like him is too involved with his own drive and desires to consider the feelings or needs of others, or even to know that others have feelings or needs important enough to be considered.

My father was intelligent and he was interested in ideas; he even had a creative turn of mind, but he had little education. If he had wished to or thought of it or believed in it, my grandfather could have sent him away to school, and he might then have accomplished something with his life that he could have taken pride in; but such a notion would never have occurred to my grandfather, and it is unlikely that my father, or any of his other children, even if the possibility had occurred to them, would have had the nerve to suggest it. As Grandpa had never gone to school, felt the need of it, or suffered from the lack of it, he saw no value in it, and I don't imagine it was ever considered. My father was left to spend his life farming and horse trading in pale imitation of his father, and, throughout it all, never quite daring to succeed at anything.

He had his visions. He would sit on the front steps and tell me his plans. He was going to the cattle auctions in Meridian and get forty calves. He would turn the old Ray place into pasture—it only needed mending that fence across the creek—and by fall we'd have a new herd of beef cattle, and he was going to build a big new house, the biggest in the area, on that rise over toward the Dearman forty, and cut a road into it through the low ground across from the church. Such schemes would spin out as simply and as surely designed as a spider's web (and with a similar substantiality), and I would believe them, as, for the moment, would he, but when the time came to make the first move, he would fall into depression or into anger and his plans would be smothered and swallowed up in an outburst of his old sense of outrage. He had a great need to love and be loved, and I suspect that Grandpa never knew or suspected, or even realized there was any reason to know or suspect, anything about that.

When my youngest brother was born, the last of nine children and my father's third son, he gave him a name without consulting anyone, or even telling my mother until it was recorded. He named him William Preston Cooper II in honor of his father.

His feelings of tenderness or of vulnerability frightened him, and he experienced them as weakness and a source of shame. Yet they were a part of what one valued in him. Once he was visiting in Meridian when a child became lost in the neighborhood. He joined the search party and was in the group that came upon the drowned body of the little boy. He was so disturbed that he left off what he was doing and came home. Afterward he felt compelled to talk about it, to relive it. "The little chap," he would say, "was just about the size of Harry"—Harry was my younger brother—and his voice would choke, his eyes cloud over, and his hands shake. One felt for him then; one was moved by that sweetness in him.

The surprising thing, really, is that he loved as freely as he did. He adored my mother and he adored each of his children. His passion for us was intense and personal, involved and possessive —especially possessive. He did not like my mother to see anyone, she was to remain at home, she was not to have friends, and she was, above all, to avoid contact with her relatives, though, oddly, he adored them, too. He liked to visit her mother and dropped by her house very often, but God help my mother if she went over to Grandma's to help out when she was ill. He seemed overjoyed if my grandmother or my mother's sisters came to see us; he would be affectionate, at his most charming and amusing, inspired in his storytelling and in his playfulness, but he did not want any of them to have a moment alone with my mother. He would, if he could, have kept her locked in her room for the duration, and when such visits were over, a kind of paranoia would set in. He would accuse my mother of plotting with them for his downfall in whatever project he was then dreaming of. "I knew when you were all in the kitchen together that you were up to something."

When my older sisters were still at home, and as they reached dating ages, the appearance of any boy on the scene became an occasion of crisis. In his eyes they were never good enough, either in character or background; a stranger, listening, would have thought, judging from his attacks on the boys' pedigrees, that it was a matter of state concern, that we were in the direct line of ascension to all the major thrones of Europe. The girls were as well behaved as anyone could wish for, entirely circumspect, without any hint of wildness, and the young men who courted them were eminently respectable and admirable, but my father would first brood about it, then get into one of his tempers, shouting and hurling accusations, and finally make threats.

Once the girls married, however, he did an about-face and praised his sons-in-law most highly. He was rather proud of each of them, and would boast about them to the neighbors. "My son-in-law Allen Roby [or Roger Graham, or Tom Crawford] came to see me last Sunday," he would say, as if the visit had been a matter between the two of them, and as if there were something complimentary to him in it.

My father first saw my mother when she was twelve and he was twenty, and he said then that he would marry her as soon as she was old enough. He went away to Panama for two years, came back, and decided she was old enough.

I have beside my desk three pictures of her; the first one was taken in 1905 and it does not seem strange to refer to that nine-year-old as my mother, for in that child's face is the same inner serenity, the same strength of character, the same blend of poise and feminine containment that persisted throughout her life and that remains in the white-haired, porcelain-skinned, blue-eyed lady of the third picture, taken by myself a few years before her death at seventy-six.

It is there, too, in the calm, open face of the fourteen-year-old bride. Under the enormous upturned flower basket of a hat, there is the same delicate countenance with its own soft secret. She seems to be thinking her own thoughts, and yet her eyes gaze out into the world without apprehension. One can read into them some awareness that there is mystery in life, a knowledge that there are always various possibilities and choices to be made. But, along with that, one also senses in them a certainty that somehow one day will follow another, circumstance will follow circumstance, and each will be dealt with as it arrives with whatever resources are available at the time. One senses a confidence that always she will do her best without regret or complaint, and an expectation that that best will be sufficient; that, further, it will all add up to a lifetime of some meaning and of some consequence. There is an acceptance of life and of the wayward contradictions of living that is almost Oriental.

Each of her children had something of my father's hysteria in his or her nature, and my mother was something like the calm in the middle of the storm. She brought one back to reality. Her voice was rarely raised, but her observing eye was full-visioned and unbiased, and her grasp of the main argument was quiet, clear, and complete. She had brain and character and concern (and, incidentally, a good head for business), and those were good anchors to hold onto.

She was the strength of the family, the pillar around which it revolved.

I will, throughout this book, use the masculine pronoun very often, just as I will speak of the race of man—man has done this or that; man must prevail; man has genius in his head—and I would like to state loudly and clearly that when I say "man" or when I use "he," I mean "man and woman" and I mean "he and she"; I do not so state each time because the use of the masculine form is an ancient and historical one, dating from a time when power, both political and personal, was indeed invested in the male, and it is a literary form with which I am comfortable. But that does not mean that I think men are stronger, brighter, more worthy, more steadfast, or more promising than women. I am under no illusion that the history of mankind is the history of men alone, that the accomplishments we celebrate, the progress we claim, is due to the work of men alone, or that the future of mankind depends upon the efforts, skill, and talents of women any less than upon those of men. I learned very early in life that those attributes I found admirable, such as courage, truth, compassion, sacrifice, wisdom, integrity of purpose and fullness of heart, have nothing to do with gender, and I rejoice that those qualities of tenderness, vulnerability, and gentleness once considered inappropriate for the male sex are now qualities that they can admit to without embarrassment or apology. I learned something about that in my home, where my mother's quiet strength stood in sharp contrast to the blustering weakness of my father.

She was, undeniably, all those things considered feminine: pretty, careful of her appearance, maternal, loving to her children, and supportive of her husband, but she was also dependable, protective, reassuring, resourceful, and stable.

We sometimes forget that this matter of turning the women of the household into pampered, weak, delicate, mindless, and frivolous creatures, or pretending that they are something like that, has not been consistent practice throughout the ages, nor was it the custom on the farm. Like fine, impressive mansions, exaggerated, fussy and colorful fashions, and elaborate, ritualistic manners, it has been mainly a sign and symbol of periods of prosperity. When we were a nation of farmers or pushing our frontiers westward, clearing land, settling homesteads, and fighting Indians, the women labored, fought, and built alongside the men, and, if the men fell, the stalwart widows snatched up the guns, the hoes, the plows, the authority, and the command, and held their dominions with sturdy and steadfast grip.

It was the well-married granddaughters of those hardy women who became the swooning playthings of the Victorian households, the decorative possessions and sources of flattery to the patresfamilias of that era. It came to be a source of pride, a sign of success, an indication of power and prosperity, that one's wife did not have to do anything more exhausting than needlepoint or playing the spinet. Her uncertain health, delicate sensibility, refined manners, obsessive morality, studied ignorance, and utter dependency were cultivated for the sake of his self-esteem, the respect of his fellows, and his prestige in the community, not dissimilar in nature to the gingerbread on his castle, the flower in his Prince Albert lapel, the sleekness of coat and swiftness of foot of his team of horses, and his rating on the stock exchange.

As for my mother, I had occasion enough to observe her coolness under pressure, her courage in the face of adversity. There were even times when there was a home to defend, and defend it she did. I remember her standing fearlessly at the front door with a rifle and ordering off the land a sinister stranger who had appeared out of nowhere. Another time, when a snake was discovered in the attic, she simply climbed up there and shot it.

She could, on the hottest day of the year, bathe and powder her face and go out to sit in the swing, looking for all the world as cool and collected as if she'd never had to lift a hand to help herself.

She was not without physical vanity, in spite of the treasured lavender ribbon from a box of candy she'd once won for being the most modest girl in half a dozen counties; she'd always been told that she was beautiful and rather came to expect it. "Well, Jennie, you've got five beautiful daughters, but not one of them will ever be as pretty as you are," I've heard people tell her in the presence of those pretty daughters, and though there would be a mild disavowal for the sake of form, such compliments did not displease. She was not even above repeating them for you if you had not been there to hear them when they were uttered.

She was completely and simply herself, always and all ways the same, totally without guile, pretense, or artifice. She was incapable of affection, and other people's airs and graces made her laugh. She was discreet and understated, and, unlike the rest of the family, not likely to volunteer criticisms, flattery, or judgments. Asked for an opinion, she gave an honest one, considerately stated, devoid of exaggerations or persuasive adjectives, and her view usually took in all the relevant possibilities.

She had the rare wisdom not to try to hold onto her children, and, consequently, by turning them loose bound to her forever their affection and respect. She rarely tried to influence her children to change a course of action that they were determined on. She let them live their own lives and make their own mistakes. California was a long way from home when I decided to go to school there, and the theatre was an unpromising institution with which to cast one's lot, but not a word was said in opposition to either.

By the time I discovered books about King Arthur and his knights and other tales of chivalry—a world I would immediately claim as my own; like Miniver Cheevy, I missed the medieval grace of iron clothing—I was ready to view myself as her champion, defending her against the fire-breathing dragon who huffed and puffed around our house.

Apart from my Oedipal feelings (sorry, but there it is; what other term can one use?) the main problem lay in my father's plans for me.

He formed them early; perhaps they were there before I was. I would be his revenge against the world; more than that, I was to be his vindication. "You listen to me, boy, and I'll make you the youngest Goddamned governor Mississippi ever had," he used to say, his eyes gazing off, across the unpromising present, into a glorious future. "When you're twenty-one, I'm going to run you for sheriff. Four years after that for the legislature."

Now I had no objection to the plan. I was all in favor of it. The problem came to be in the motives and in the methods. By the time I was old enough to listen to the Sunday school lessons, I had become obsessed with a sense of historic mission. I was going

to save the world. Nothing less than that. I did not doubt that
I had been somehow set apart for that purpose.

I might doubt myself; I did doubt myself. I doubted my
strength, my ability, my steadfastness, my capacity for self-sac-
rifice, but I did not doubt my destiny. That I was in some way
special seemed clear enough to me. There was no other boy
among my acquaintances, aged six or eight or ten or twelve, of
whom it was said, "That boy's going to be President someday,"
or "He's a born preacher; he'll be greater than Billy Sunday," or
"I'd give a million dollars to have a boy like that." Such things
were said to my father by the fathers of my schoolmates and
repeated boastfully by him at the dinner table. I knew that the
teachers at school took a particular interest in me, that they liked
to sit and talk with me during recess periods. I could see that other
children my age did not share my interests, or know what I knew,
think as I thought, or feel as I felt. Reading, for them, was a
matter of recognizing that Jack can run fast, I can run fast too,
and that adding 2 apples and 2 apples would get them 4 apples,
while to me it had to do with logic and knowledge and discovery,
a key to a door behind which lay the explosive hunger of my mind.

The precocious child soon finds out that he is precocious, and
it is not an unmixed blessing for him, which explains the unpleasant behavior that sometimes is identified with it. My son Carter
was an extraordinary child and he used to say of his friends with
some puzzlement, "Bill doesn't know about Julius Caesar," or
"He tried to mix Roman soldiers in with Crusaders!" Once we
were going through the Metropolitan Museum and Carter was
having a marvelous time pointing out things to Anderson: "That's
from Egypt and they were about five hundred years before the
Romans, and this is . . ." We noticed a lady following us about
and she asked me, "Is this some kind of scientific experiment or
something?"

But he really learned that he was unusual from taxi drivers. We would be returning from a movie (at five he sat several times through the Russian *War and Peace*) or other cultural experiences; he would be bubbling over with excitement and chattering away—he had the diction and vocabulary of a Philadelphia lawyer —"I think Shakespeare was right," he might say of something in *Henry V*, for instance, and the driver would turn around and ask, "How old is that kid?" That didn't have to happen too many times before he realized that he could make them turn around, and since it's only one step from the thought to the deed, he would begin conversations in taxis that I knew were for the driver's benefit. Such a child realizes, too, that he's not as brilliant as they think he is, and while he likes the praise, he also begins to feel that he's a bit of a fraud. Once that happens, much of the spontaneous delight in learning goes out the window, along with innocence; the child becomes involved with the impression rather than the substance, and it's time to draw his attention to more usual fare for his age. A child needs very much to fit in with his peers.

I felt an obligation about whatever specialness it was that was my lot, and that obligation alternately thrilled and frightened me. I doubted my willingness to fulfill it, and what I prayed for—and that fervently—was that I should be dedicated enough, compassionate enough, and moral enough to meet the task ahead of me. I was aware of my weaknesses; I knew myself sometimes to be selfish, conceited, greedy for admiration, ambitious for myself and scornful of others. I knew that I was often silly and vain, that my thinking was fuzzy and unclear, my knowledge superficial, and my motives mixed. It was pretty hard to accept these frailties as right and natural in a Messiah. It did not square with my passion to banish all injustice, all suffering, all pain and distress, to heal all wounds, to lead the way into a full, rich, and joyful world in which all men lived together in peace and brotherhood. I submitted myself to my own rueful inquisition, and found myself wanting.

I asked myself, as we were taught to do in church, "Would Christ do what I'm doing? Would he feel in his heart what I feel in my heart?" and, too often, the only possible answer was that he would not.

Papa did not know my feelings. Nobody did. It's not the kind of thing you mention around the schoolyard. The child learns to dissemble and conceal his insecurities, and I concentrated upon remaining poised.

My dismay came from the crass materialism of his motives, and probably from some unconscious or unacknowledged fear that I shared his materialism. As sheriff I could build him a road, throw favors his way, and give him a special status among the men who sat on the benches on Courthouse Square on Saturday afternoons. As governor—well, there must be a lot that a governor could do for his father, and there must be benches around the statehouse square, too, with men sitting on them that he could talk to.

That wasn't so bad, really. There are worse things than a sheriff building a road across his father's property, and that worse thing for me was the callous way he advised me to set about attaining our goal. When I, as a twelve-year-old, would be asked in the absence of the minister to speak to the congregation, or when one of the town fathers would tell my father that I was a good Christian boy, my father would say to me, "That's just fine, Son. You keep that up. You've got the church vote sewed up right now." Or, if I brought a friend home from school, my father would say, "His daddy carries a lot of weight down there in De Soto, and you need to get that crowd behind you."

I felt a terrible shame in that, as if I were choosing friends with an ulterior purpose, as if I were doing and saying those things that would build up some gainful image, but I was never quite able to confront him with that shame. I simply stopped responding, except for the response that silence gives. How could a son talk to such a father about moral convictions, explain his sense of what was right and wrong, when to him anybody who engaged in such talk without some selfish purpose could only be a fool?

The end result of it has been that ever since then, not only have I been unable to say anything I do not fully mean, but it has been virtually impossible for me to promote myself for positions in the world that I felt myself to be quite suited for. When I was an actor, and knew many influential people in the theatre, I could never bring myself to ask anybody for a job. Worse than that, I wasn't even able to audition; there was too much supplication in the act of trying out, and my performance, under the stress of auditions, would be no more capable than it had been on the afternoon of plowing in the wet ground. When I got jobs, it was always from somebody who had seen me in some other play, and asked me to play a part without the requirement of auditioning. Even so, I felt compelled to list all the reasons I might be found wanting in the role, hoping to be persuaded of my own qualifications. Sometimes, to my distress, I was taken at my word, and the offer would be withdrawn. In luckier times, I allowed myself to be persuaded. In Hollywood, when Peter Glenville asked me to write my first screenplay for him at a salary many times anything I'd ever earned as an actor, I sat in his living room and tried to convince him that I was the wrong choice for the assignment.

I've been stuck with some image of myself as a sort of Thomas Jefferson puttering around his estate at Monticello politely protesting when the committee comes to tell him that only he can save the country. Though, oddly enough, once the matter of motives is behind and it's clear that I've made no aggressive move to win the honor, once my crass ambition has been denied and my scruples overcome, I can enter into whatever assignment has been thrust upon me with dispatch, confidence, and an iron conviction that I know exactly how it is to be done.

Politics attracted me and I would have liked holding office, but by the time I was in my teens I had taken the wrong position on almost any issue that was likely to come up, and was writing letters to the newspapers to state those positions. It must have been clear even to so single-minded a man as my father that, holding the views I held, a future for me in local politics was highly unlikely, though he may have thought that once my growing pains were done with I would, in his phrase, "straighten out and fly right." He said of me at one point, "He hasn't been the same since he read that *Uncle Tom's Cabin.*"

There is an ironic footnote that I might add to this account of my father's frustrated political plans for me. I was visited in New York a few years ago by two influential Mississippi citizens with a plan that I move back there and become involved in state life with the intention of running for governor. One of the reasons that they gave for my acceptability was that my views on civil rights fitted in with the new enlightened image of that growing and progressive state. I wonder what my father would have said to that. Actually, I suppose I know. He would have decided that I'd been shrewder and craftier all along than he'd ever suspected.

Now, before I leave this too bright and too clean portrait of my youthful self, I must fill in the picture by describing a dark streak of compulsive meanness toward my brother that somewhat mars my record. Nobody can be more sneaky than a "good" boy.

According to all reports, I was as sweet a child as ever was. Anybody within a radius of seven miles from our farm can testify to that. I was a model of deportment and held up as an example by local parents to their riotous boys. My sister Grace said to me once, "Why, there was never a child in the world as adored as you were! And it wasn't just us. Everybody did!"

All right, but I had one flaw.

My brother Harry was born when I was five. Up to then I'd had no problem that couldn't be fixed, but he arrived and wouldn't go away. My sister Janice had come in between, but that was all right; she was a girl and she soon followed me around as admiring as the rest. But Harry was another boy, and that was a terrible blow from which I was never to recover. My own birth had come after four girls, one of whom died just before I was born, and as a cousin put it, "If you'd been another Christ child, there couldn't have been more rejoicing." As if that weren't enough, I got diphtheria when I was a year old and for a long time it was expected that I was to die. Ladies used to tell me how they'd knelt around my bed praying that I be spared. I recovered and there was more rejoicing. All that's heady stuff for a youngster; it doesn't exactly keep him from feeling that he's one of a kind; I was, in fact, treated like something pretty special and I came to take my "specialness" for granted. With that kind of attention it is not surprising that a child could manage to have a sunny disposition. Then, since I never knew when to stop, I topped myself by getting an unprecedented second case of diphtheria a year later and we went through the whole process again, and everything went swimmingly until that second boy appeared.

It didn't help matters that he looked exactly like me, either. Somehow, I didn't find that flattering. And Papa wasted no time transferring his attention to the newcomer; maybe he was tired of sharing me with my local fans, or, more probably, it was apparent to him at once that this son would be the companion he wanted, for in no time at all little Harry was as tough as a bullet, and was following my father around the farm like an ambitious understudy. For him there would be no lolling around in swings reading books and amusing the womenfolk with droll stories; he would be an outdoor type and, I believe too, he paid careful attention to all the advice Papa gave him.

I had one last experience of total approval from my father, just as Harry was getting his foothold, when I came home from my first day of school, which happened to have been on my fifth birthday. I told Papa that it was fun; Estelle Armstead (seven) and Darleen Tuck (eight) had played a game in which they took turns dropping their pencils down the front of my overalls and then reaching in and feeling around to find them. I don't think I was ever to give my father as proud a moment as that again. He got as much pleasure from it as he would if it had happened to him, and each time he told it, which was as often as he could find a listener, he enjoyed it all over again.

So Harry moved in. My method of dealing with him was sly, and it reveals the real defect in my otherwise sterling character. My purpose was to discredit him. It was not enough that I be thought brilliant; he must be thought stupid. It was not enough that I be considered to be of good character; his must be shown up as disgraceful. And he was most cooperative in the endeavor. He had a violent temper, and I only needed to drop a few innocent words that he didn't understand into a sentence to make him suspect that he'd been insulted; or I might say lightly, "Harry, I don't guess you're doing long division yet" (which he obviously wasn't since I'd only just begun it and he was five years younger), and he would, right on cue, fly off the handle and attack me with whatever weapon was at hand. Once he started, there was no turning back. The pattern was that as soon as he attacked, I would wrestle him to the ground (I was, after all, considerably bigger than he was) and calmly sit on him as he lay sputtering and spitting, red with rage, while Janice went to fetch Mama. I was careful to have Janice there. She made an excellent witness; fairly and impartially, she would report to Mama who hit first.

Siblings of the same sex are bound to be rivals, I suppose, and parents have to make clear their love for each child and see that they understand that the differences between them are sources of pleasure, rather than failings in one or the other. Carter is intellectual, thoughtful, sensitive, gentle, fastidious, subtle, and very aware of everything around him. He likes reading, talking, and time to think his thoughts. Anderson is a freckle-faced Huck Finn, fun-loving, witty, clever, quick, energetic, and inventive. He should live in the country, on a farm, with trees to climb, a river to play in, and all sorts of animals. He's very much an outdoor boy. He passionately loves dogs, mice, rabbits, horses—anything that moves, and the wilder it is, the better. He sat one night watching Sam, his beloved snake, curling around his hand, marveling that this wild creature actually belonged to him, and he asked it, with wonder in his voice, "Sam, is dis all a dream?"

He is a diligent worker and will accept from himself nothing less than his best. Trying to draw a horse, he will impatiently tear up attempt after attempt because the legs aren't coming right; he is not interested in being told that horses' legs are next to impossible to get right; he will keep at it until he is satisfied with the result. At five when he was given a camera, he turned all his considerable concentration toward learning to use it correctly, and his pictures are more carefully composed than those of many adults. His sly sense of humor is totally his own and somehow wise beyond his years. When Carter said that he had been kissed by Frank Sinatra as an infant, Anderson said, "Aw, wasn't I ever kissed by anybody famous—Little Orphan Annie, or somebody like that?" To watch television with him is a joy. His droll comments, particularly about the artificial enthusiasms and unlikely concerns of the performers in commercials, are devastating. A born mimic, he uses economy of gesture and precise vocal inflections to show how a German nurse in a restaurant bullied her charges into eating all their Wiener schnitzel. He will mime the angry astonishment of the show-off at the skating rink whose legs suddenly flew out from under him, or the languid and innocent lasciviousness of the teenage flirt tottering on her platform shoes in the school cafeteria. He is a determined little fellow. When we went to the Mayan ruins in Yucatán, the gigantic pyramid at Uxmal, which seemed to go straight up into the air, frightened all of us, but Anderson refused to be swayed by his fear. While Gloria, Carter, and I watched anxiously, he set out with Chris and, like a cautious little spider, scaled the 365 steps to reach the top.

Children have a dignity and bravery that come near to breaking the heart. The skills and information they have to acquire must seem monumental to them. There is the threat of all the vast unknown. The whole world towers over them. I think of Anderson strolling with me at intermission time in the huge intimidating space of the New York State Theatre promenade, his small frame dwarfed by its soaring height, but there he is, walking tall, with an ease that is more public pose than true assurance, with a bit of swagger even, and he chats casually as if we were of the same stature, assuming a kind of manliness, trying it on for size. I think of him at five leaving home for the first time without any of us to go away to Disney World with his friend Carter Burden, looking big and determined and small and forlorn all at the same time. I think of Carter at four, lying in the intensive-care room after major surgery with tubes in his nose, side, and arms. When a nurse approached him, he would lift his fingers, the only part of his body he could move, and say, "Wait a minute, nurse." Startled, she would ask, "What is it, Carter?" and he would answer, "Tell me what you're going to do and I can help you."

I remember hearing my mother say that she loved all her children the same and thinking, "Of course she says that, but it can't be true. Each one is different. A parent must like one more than the other." Now I understand. Each of my sons delights me in quite different, but equal, ways. Carter and I recognized ourselves in each other from the very beginning. We think alike and often read each other's thoughts, communicating with glances and half-smiles without the necessity of words. For instance: He was about three and we were walking along the street when a man approached using a cane. Just as he was even with us Carter asked, "Why is that man walking with a cane?" I waited until the man moved out of earshot and said, "It's all right to ask that, but we

don't ask it when the man can hear it, do we?" Carter said, "No,"
and, to make sure he understood, I asked, "Why not?" and he
replied, "Because it might hurt his feelings." O.K. That point
made, we moved on. At the next corner, as we waited to cross the
street, a little old lady, playing, as some little old ladies do, the
part of little old lady, looked at him and asked with a sweetness
she'd learned from the movies, "Is that a little boy or a little girl?"
Dumb. He looked nothing at all like a girl. His hair was cut like
a boy's, and besides that, you don't call children little, not if you
have manners, so I replied with coldness in my voice, "*He* is a
big boy." Carter recognized immediately that I was putting her
in her place. He knew she was old enough to know the lesson he
had just learned, so he spoke up, enunciating clearly and distinctly
so that his purpose was unmistakable. "Daddy," he said, "is that
lady a midget?"

With Anderson I have a separate but equal relationship. He
used to say to me, almost nightly and just after dinner, "Let's go
to the pizza place," not because he was really hungry for a slice
of pizza but because those jaunts were something between the
two of us. It gave him a chance to talk about whatever was on his
mind, but more than that, it was an opportunity for one-to-one,
man-to-man contact without having to share that connection
with an older brother who'd managed to get there first.

I know that both boys admire me. I see it, and their teachers
and others have told me so, but their admiration for me cannot
be any more than the admiration I have for each of them; and
when we walk together, they're not the only ones walking tall.

I want them to respect and enjoy each other's differences just
as we as parents respect and enjoy those differences. If Anderson
hates something that Carter likes, then Carter must not take that
as an attack upon his taste and judgment, and vice versa. Actually,
apart from the fact that they would like to kill each other, they
get along well.

They are aware of the parallels between their relationship and that of Harry and me. It has become a kind of joke between us. Carter has the impulse to do to Anderson exactly the kind of thing I have just described my doing to Harry, but the difference is that both of them will recognize what is happening and they can laugh about it. Carter will start to say something that asserts his superiority, all meekness and sweet interest: "Anderson, are you still on the first reader?" Then he will catch my eye, grin sheepishly, and say, "I know. Just like you did to Harry." And old Anderson holds his own. In the beginning he would listen to such a performance of Carter's for a little while without any comment; then he would back off, take a big swing, and lunge for him.

My wife and I worked hard at preparing Carter for Anderson's debut. There was lots of jolly talk about baby Napoleon in Mummy's tummy and listening to hear his (or her) heartbeats or feeling for his (or her) kicks. Everything was explained and Carter was all eagerness. When it happened, though, the wind went right out of his sails. We have a photograph of Gloria holding the new infant while Carter stands beside her with the most awful sick grin spread painfully across his face. He was, for the first few months, subdued and shocked, and we spent all our time cheering him up, showering him with attention, trying to show that we loved him as much as ever, but he knew that he had lost that special status as the adored only, and nothing we promised about future playmates could restore that. Other photographs of them together in that first year tell the same story, with Anderson, the displacer, sitting sleek, fat, and satisfied, a twinkle in his eyes and a smug smile on his puss, looking directly into the camera, while Carter, affecting elaborate disinterest, fixes his gaze in an opposite direction, and nervously chews the insides of his lips. Once he told the nurse that he wanted to tiptoe into the room where the baby was sleeping, in order to fetch some toy or other, and May agreed. A moment later she heard a sharp scream from Anderson, and rushed into the nursery to find a startled Carter standing over the baby with his hand still upraised. He had seen his chance to get a good lick in while Anderson was asleep, figuring nobody would know about it; it hadn't occurred to him that "it" would wake up and sound an alarm.

In the beginning I would talk to Carter about the golden opportunity he had at that time to influence Anderson in the right direction. Anderson was then full of admiration for this older brother who could walk and run and play while Anderson lay watching, his eyes following Carter everywhere he went as if he longed to join him in his activities. I pointed out to Carter that if he took advantage of that, if he would share with him now, and be cooperative and helpful, then Anderson would, later on, be the same way, whereas if Carter did the natural thing and was grabby and kept on saying "That's mine" when Anderson crawled over and picked up something, he could expect Anderson to copy him when he got bigger, for he would have been taught by Carter's example that that was the way to be. Carter understood and he would nod in agreement, but the effort was too much. The sacrifices were all in the present and the rewards in a future too remote. Present power is much more pleasurable than the promise of future peace. "My castle is bigger than Anderson's," he would say of the two piles of blocks they had been stacking up, cutting his eyes around to me to see if I'd recognized the intent. Once he stopped halfway in just that sentence, and finished lamely, ". . . we've both built interesting castles, haven't we, Anderson?" Then he smiled his dazzling smile and said, "You see, Daddy, I'm learning."

I might truthfully say that I set out to be a good father because my father was a bad father, but is it really true? I suspect that in saying it I might be quite wrong. It is certainly true that his fathering did not work out pleasantly for either of us, but it may be equally true that the fact that I wanted to be a father at all comes not from his actual performance but from his original impulse. *He* wanted to be a good father. Doubtless he wanted to be a better father than his father had been to him. Probably he resolved to correct the mistakes his father had made. That I did not respond to his particular style and method came about because of his lack of perception about me, and because of his ambivalence about himself, but that he cared and was involved, that he invested himself in the relationship, was never in question. And so it may be that he gave me a great deal more than I thought I was getting at the time.

Most of the things that one wishes for in one's life turn out to be, upon attainment, little more than the muddied reflection of the dream, but in this matter of becoming a father it has been everything I ever thought it would be, only more: the richness of it, the sweetness, the fun, the fulfillment, the excitement, the day-to-day renewal. If there is anything to the notion of reincarnation, I must have done something awfully nice somewhere along the line to be generously rewarded in this way.

What Went Wrong?

I live, I don't know how long;
I die, I don't know when;
I go, I don't know where:
I am amazed that I can be
so cheerful!
—*Epitaph of Martius*
of Biberbach, 1498

When my generation was young, our parents could reasonably expect that we would live in a world that bore some resemblance to their own, as their world resembled that of their parents. They assumed that there would be differences, but those differences would be in the direction of the better: they would be corrections of the defects of their times. For this they were willing to work hard, and because of this they passionately believed in providing more education than they had been given. They were an optimistic generation. They never doubted that the future would bring better opportunities, better living conditions, better governments. Were we not learning more every day? Improving ourselves in every way? It would be a more stable world surely—had we not made the world safe for democracy? And did not the rest of the world look to us for enlightenment? Problems were there to be solved and were solvable, and we, their children, would live in calm and in security, with the basic shape of our lives much the same as theirs.

Now, a few decades later, such assurance about the future seems as remote as the Middle Ages, as removed from us as the fervor of the Crusades. We have trouble visualizing tomorrow, much less imagining what it will be like thirty years from now, and the guesses that are made for us are not calculated to give us much ease of mind. It is not for nothing we have been flocking to that series of sequels that grew out of the first *Planet of the Apes* movie. They are fantasies, clearly, and we can enjoy their foolishness; we can even reassure ourselves by pointing out the impossibilities of the plots. But amid the absurdity is something that rings disturbingly in our heads: how impossible is the impossible?

How did it come about that in a relatively short space of time the familiarity of our world and the industructibility of its institutions are gone? Our sense of self is threatened. We stand among the ruins of our hopes, wondering who we are, what we want, and what we are expected to do. Far more educated than any people in history, we are uncertain of what we can believe in. We can't make up our minds about our worth, or even whether we have any worth. We do not know in what we can take pride or of what we should be ashamed. What can we believe in any more?

If you asked my father a simple question like "Are you going to vote for President Roosevelt?" he was likely to begin his reply with "When Uncle Jim was fighting under General Bragg in the Battle of Chickamauga . . ." and it might be hours before he got around to mention of Mr. Roosevelt's re-election. It did no good to try to hurry him through the accounts of Uncle Jim's injuries or the rain that fell on the day he returned or his attitude toward the Reconstruction era, for all those memories would be revealed, at the end of the recitation, to have been an integral part of the decision you had asked him about. My narrative style I inherited from him. I can remember, when I was in the fifth grade, handing in essays that rambled on for many pages only to reach the assigned subject in a few desperate paragraphs at the end, scribbled furiously on the school bus on the way to school. Miss Onie Acklin would return them with the comment, "Interesting, but *please* try to get to the subject!" I'm still trying, and as I stumble on, trusting more to instinct than to intellect, I'm rarely sure whether I'm digressing or laying foundations. Nevertheless, it is true that we are sometimes unable to get from one place to another except by a circuitous route. Which is by way of saying that I find I cannot get on to talking about what has happened to the family as a living institution without some examination of what has happened to us as a nation, as a people, and as individuals.

This is a large subject, deserving of more than the passing glance and quick summary that space affords us here. It involves such diverse matters as political developments, the movement of history, the influence of technology, and changes in philosophical and sociological opinions. Cursory treatment makes it hard not to oversimplify, for the complexities that underlie historic events are often not discernible until a good deal of time has passed. Still, we are, these days, taking stock, as we must; some perspective is possible; and certain things seem clear enough.

Once we as Americans believed in our country's historic destiny, and we had some justification. We began, after all, as a noble and unprecedented experiment in freedom, and we grew to feel an almost mystic sense of mission, as if we had been set apart by Divine Providence to be an example to other nations. We believed in our good intentions, and a great deal of good has grown out of that faith; but some results have not been so benign.

And in the decade of the sixties we came face to face with certain contradictions in our feelings about ourselves. We were forced to begin a painful re-examination of our motives, and this shattered complacency. We began to feel rejected by much of the rest of the world, and we were torn by a new wave of internal conflict.

We started that decade with a high optimism that was probably overeager, an incautious exuberance that had its own dangers.
It began with the inauguration as President of a young man of
intellect, wit, and grace; with talk of torches being passed to a new
generation, with a sense of high purpose and a belief in our best
possibilities. We began it with a hero and a trumpet call to
greatness. A few years later some of us would fear that we were
done forever not only with heroism but with belief itself.

In 1963 I went down to the University of Alabama to stay with
my cousin, the president of the university, during the time that
Governor Wallace made his promised gesture of standing at the
schoolhouse door to bar the entrance of two black students, a
young man and a young woman, the university had accepted. It
was an historic occasion and I wanted to be there. It is no longer
a secret that the proceedings followed a prearranged plan that had
been worked out, by emissaries, between the governor and Robert
Kennedy as Attorney General. The real significance was not what
it appeared to be on the television screen, a confrontation between the power of the federal government and that of a state,
for that issue had been settled long before by the Civil War, and
most of the participants in the drama were like nervous actors,
afraid that some other actor was going to do something that was
not in the script. The true meaning of the event was that the
students themselves, on a campus that seven years earlier, when
Autherine Lucy had been briefly enrolled, had erupted into riots
that for a time closed down the school, now behaved in the
rational, mature, and courteous manner that I associate with
Southern gentility.

The highway patrolman who had escorted the male student to
his dormitory room reported in at noon to my cousin, who was
in the kitchen with his wife frying hamburgers for the board of
trustees. (The servants, being black, were not allowed on campus
that day.) He took a cup of coffee, sat down and fanned himself
with his hat, perfectly at ease in the distinguished gathering, and

began by saying, "You know, that boy's just as bright as he can be, and he's got as good manners as you'd ever hope to see." He told us the other students had welcomed their new black classmate, offered to help him unpack, and had told him that they could all watch the events of the day on television together in the lounge that evening.

It was a moving experience for me. More than one person learned something that day. All of us, Northerners as well as Southerners, have lived with a burden of guilt for slavery and its legacy, and a new day seemed to me to be dawning in which we were learning to accept one another as human beings with equal rights to that pursuit of happiness promised in our Declaration of Independence.

A few months later came the incredible event in Dallas that shocked and numbed a nation. Each of us was shattered by it and we wept, for we were still then in touch with our feelings. We wept for the loss of a promise, not knowing that soon we were to be afraid to believe in a promise ever again. We could still hope that out of tragedy might come a drawing together for the general good, and for a while, and to some extent, something like that seemed to be happening. Then horror began to pile upon horror, and we started building a series of walls around our feelings for our own protection. We began to accept new disasters as non-events. Martin Luther King, Jr., once said, "When the history books are written in future generations, the historians will have to pause and say, 'There lived a great people—a black people—who injected new meaning and dignity into the veins of civilization'"—surely one of the noble utterances of our time—and yet when he was shot down on a Memphis balcony, we knew that terrible feeling of having been through it all before. From the moment the first news flash came, one kept oneself occupied with various small tasks in an attempt to postpone any actual recognition of what had happened. One kept one's voice steady and carried on one's conversations; one picked up the children's toys and made plans for the weekend as if the tragedy in Memphis had nothing to do with one's life. It was too soon to have to endure it all again.

In the end we had to. It *had* happened, and turning our gaze away from the television set did not keep the truth from being there, any more than turning away could keep it from happening again. We would see Bobby Kennedy's face, that face of the young and handsome warrior, lying in a pool of blood on the cold floor of a Los Angeles hotel kitchen with a bullet in his brain, and we would be curiously without surprise. By then we knew we were engaged in a cruel, useless, and unjust war, and hate, fear, suspicion, and violence had become so common a part of our lives that there was an odd air of unreality about it. So estranged had we come to feel from events that we watched such things on television screens in play and replay almost dispassionately, feeling somehow that it might be a mechanical thing—that they could as easily reverse the tape and the fallen hero would stand up and walk backward, smiling and waving, into the speech he had been making a few minutes before.

For the first time in history we saw a war up close. We sat in our living rooms and watched helicopters hovering endlessly over a scorched and scalded land, over hills and ridges that were taken yesterday and abandoned today because there was nothing there to hold. We saw our sons, just out of high school, strewn across rice fields, lying in death as peacefully as if they were sleeping. We watched ourselves laying waste a primitive land of beautiful people, and after a time it didn't matter what they told us. The generals came on the air to assure us that we were destroying villages in order to save them, and we knew that it was terribly and desperately wrong.

It has been said that the war brutalized a generation. Certainly it changed us. Whatever one's beliefs may have been about the war's rights or wrongs, one could not be untouched by the pain and despair in the faces of the young who would be called upon to bear the brunt of it. Their rebellion shocked some of us. For a long time we had talked of the threat of enemies from abroad while we ignored the problems building up at home. We were not aware of the difference between what we were and what we believed ourselves to be. We did not face the gaps that were widening between groups in the country, and we were startled to find race in conflict with race, class with class, youth with age, section with section, and the individual with the whole.

I am somewhat given to anticipating the worst. Once my father was engaged in a feud with a neighbor. It had begun long before when my mother's grandfather refused to sell my father forty acres of land that adjoined our property. This neighbor bought the land with the avowed intention of annexing our house, which sat uncomfortably near the disputed property line. When he failed at that, he planted a garden just over the line, only a few feet from our back door and a mile from his own house. Our chickens, which were allowed to roam free, naturally made themselves at home in it, and the neighbor appeared there one day with his rifle and a stool to sit on, and as each chicken set foot on his domain he shot it. My father arrived home, was not pleased, got his own rifle, and for a long time the two men stood threatening each other with their guns. It was a case, I suppose, of balance-of-power politics, for neither pulled the trigger. I was positive that they would, though—I had been warning the family for weeks that we might all be murdered in our beds—and I spent the time hanging out the window begging, "Don't do it, Papa." My mother, with wisdom born of more experience, went on about her business of getting supper ready.

My habit of predicting disaster amounts to a kind of superstition. It is my hope, I suspect, that if I present a case in its darkest form, the anger of the gods will be appeased and subsequent events will happily prove me wrong. And in the ugliest days of the sixties, with two stepsons at my house about to reach draft age, my hope for the future was at its lowest. I did what I could, which consisted mostly of campaigning against the war and in behalf of those peace candidates who opposed it. The problems had become so large and the individual so small that too many people were shrugging their shoulders and asking, "What's the use?"

Yet even then I realized that all times probably seem desperate to those who are living through them. Very likely we always feel as if we are standing at a fearful fork in the road and surely the paths ahead are always shrouded in uncertainty.

The sense of impotence that seems to be at the real core of our present dilemma is derived not so much from political situations as from the overwhelming changes, social, spiritual, and cultural, that are brought about by a technological age; and recent developments in the political area indicate that we are far less impotent than we had begun to think. We have, in turning against the war, and in facing up to the corruption of the Watergate scandals, asserted ourselves as a self-determining people.

Some of us, especially the young, responded too quickly to the crises by writing off the validity of all our traditional assertions and values, by throwing out *everything* we once believed in. What is needed, surely, is a continuing examination of our inherited beliefs, a sorting out of those that are enduring and constructive and a discarding of those that do not stand up to scrutiny.

We could do worse than to remind ourselves, in this process of self-criticism in which we are now engaged, that many of the failings for which we hold ourselves accountable are relatively new in history. There was a time, after all, when it did not occur to soldiers to question the morality of the wars they were sent to. There are countries today in which corruption in government circles is taken for granted and in which people do not feel responsible for the poor, the old, the sick, or for those who are victims of an indifferent society. We have grown to take our humanistic ideals and expectations for granted and we judge ourselves severely in the light of those ideals.

I believe that we are asking more questions than ever before and not assuming that we already have the answers. Man is an inquiring animal. We come into the world asking "Why?" and "How?" and we are never satisfied. Yet when questions are honestly asked, surely we are on the road to honest answers.

We are having to remake our world at a time when it is not easy to believe that we count, that we make a difference.

We are having to rethink and re-examine what we believe in, what we are willing to live by, what we will pass on to our children.

My youngest son will be only seventeen in George Orwell's brutally prophetic year of 1984. We cannot anticipate the problems those children will face. We can only be sure that their lives will be infinitely more different from ours than ours were from those of our parents. How can we peer into that darkness and prepare them to deal with the unknown? What can we give them that will help? We face these questions every day, and we have no answers yet. We can only teach them some flexibility, instill in them some degree of adaptability, tell them what we have found to be of value, and hope that it will be of use under unplanned and unplanable conditions.

All this was once spelled out for us by church, state, school, and custom. The systems were quite clearly laid out, and you conformed to the one you were born to or found another one elsewhere that fitted your needs. Now the old rules do not always apply nor the old slogans always suffice. Familiar explanations and justifications do not always serve. Dogma is dead. We are, in a sense, freer than ever, and that freedom can be terrifying.

We used to believe that we were a part of a long process that was self-perpetuating and that took us along with it. It was called Progress. We used to have roots: roots in a time, a place, a family, and a community. We used to have heroes, legendary, national, or personal, on which we could model ourselves. These told us who we were, what we were capable of, what we could expect, and what we were to do.

Let us see what has happened.

7

A Question of Progress

"Now, here, you see, it takes all the running you can do, to keep in the same place. If you want to get somewhere else, you must run at least twice as fast as that!" —LEWIS CARROLL

"Striving to better, oft we mar what's well." —SHAKESPEARE

To begin with, the chief enemy is progress. Fifty years ago that would have been a sacrilegious statement and I might have been hanged publicly for making it. We were celebrating a century of progress and looking forward to the millennium. But we have gone too far too fast. We've been much too clever, too smart for our own britches, as we used to say; and our very inventiveness has betrayed us.

A hundred years ago miracles started becoming commonplace. It must have been a thrilling day in which one first heard about the invention of the telephone. How incredible it must have seemed that one could pick up an instrument in New York and, with the aid of a piece of wire, converse with a friend in Washington! How skeptical people must have been, and what a promising thing it must have seemed! How cheerful a place the future must have looked. Doubt became a sin. And they were right in so looking forward, for it was a miraculous thing that men had brought about. I am myself still astonished by the telephone and by electric light, and by radio, to say nothing of television, for I lived the first fifteen years of my life without them, except for a battery-powered radio that sometimes functioned. The nearest telephone was three miles away at Mr. Tuttle's house—the line went no farther—and if a doctor had to be called, my father saddled the horse and rode over to Tuttle's to shout our emergency into that novel contraption. Electric light didn't reach rural areas in my part of Mississippi until wartime, and by then I was living in New Orleans. When our radio was functioning, or when Cicero White's did, neighbors would walk miles to gather around the sputtering and crackling box to hear *The Grand Ole Opry* from Nashville, Tennessee, on Saturday nights, or *Amos 'n' Andy*, or the Joe Louis–Max Schmeling fight. They seemed like great blessings then and they seem like blessings now, but it was the beginning of the loss of something.

The radio brought to us artists and comedians we would never have known otherwise, but it began to take away from us something of our own. I can remember, before Cicero White bought his radio with his veteran's bonus money, when we used to gather at Tom Hayes's place and listen to the Hayes family sing; they were one of those musical families that used to happen along; families in which each member, as he came into the world, uttered a musical cry, unlike those ungifted ones of us who squealed and squalled in the usual way. Hayeses never had to study music; they picked it up out of the air. And they sang for the joy of singing. It was alive, real, personal, there, in the flesh; it was theirs —their creation—and it was ours, because they, the Hayeses, were ours, part of us, and we all gathered together in enjoyment of this thing that they did. When we started our Saturday nights with *The Grand Ole Opry*, with Minnie Pearl, Uncle Dave Macon, Bill Monroe and the Bluegrass Boys, Roy Acuff, the Carter family, we added something new; their music expressed something of the pain and some of the simple pleasures of country people's lives. The songs were about hard work, about death, about faith, and about love betrayed. In the nasal twang of the singing, its plaintive cry, the harsh rural accents, the fierce bravado of the humor, we felt the hard realities of our world reflected. Gone were the pure lyrical voices one associates with earlier folk music, and in their place was a pinched, almost ugly, sound, with a piercing sort of whine in it, as if life were too cruel and desperate and precious a matter to be musical about. They were the songs of a people who lived close to the soil and they sprang from the heart.

We gained a great deal when we began to listen to the radio, but at a cost. Out of necessity, families used to sit around and entertain each other. They made up games, puzzles, riddles; they did things: stringing popcorn, pulling taffy, building a swing, sewing a quilt, making a doll out of a corncob and piece of rag, talking. Most of all, talking. We told stories. People ask why it is that every Southern town of any size, and some of almost no size, have produced published writers, many of them major voices in American letters, and the answer is clear. Southerners have a tradition of telling stories to each other, or they used to, anyway. I can remember sitting, still and quiet, hunkered down on the floor next to my father's chair while he talked. It could be about almost anything, and it might be true or it might not be. He could tell about a hunting trip and you felt it all with him, the darkness of the night, the deep silence of the woods, the excitement of the chase, the barking of the dogs, the life-and-death drama of it. It might be about some escapade in Panama, where he'd spent some years as a youth, or a tale about his uncles or grandparents or some local character from long ago; sometimes they were richly comic —scraps come back to me:

A pig falls into the vat of somebody's whiskey still—was it Papa's? his father's? it doesn't matter—and the moonshiner, wondering whether the whiskey has been ruined, decides to test it on an unsuspecting neighbor. The neighbor takes a long pull on the bottle, wipes his mouth with satisfaction, and beams: "Damn, Emmett, if that ain't the best whiskey I ever tasted. Got an unusual kind of flavor. Sort of a hog whang to it."

Or it might be family history; he had a great fund of stories about his family. Once a mild and respectable-looking lady came to see him. She was working on one of those WPA writers projects and she had been assigned the task of writing about local history. She wanted information about a great-uncle of my father's named Jim Bull, who had been, to put it mildly, a somewhat colorful character. He had killed a surprising number of people in quarrels of one kind or another. On one occasion he shot a man for swearing in front of ladies, a serious offense in his day. "One thing about Uncle Jim," my father said to our visitor, "he wouldn't stand for no bad talk in front of the womenfolk." At another time he was insulted by a man on a train and he picked up the offender —he was a man of remarkable strength—and pitched him into the firebox. Jim Bull was not considered a criminal, or even a bad man. I should think it unlikely that he was ever arrested for any of these acts. One must remember that those were remote days, frontier times almost, and men were expected to take care of themselves. It was a weak man, indeed, who called the law in to settle his disputes. In keeping with the rest of his life, Uncle Jim's death was a violent one. He was in a train wreck; the train turned over and he was pinned under it; steam was escaping on him, scalding him to death. He took out his pocket knife and began cutting his own legs off in an attempt to escape the steam. The earnest lady from the WPA was quite impressed by these and other tales my father told her during the course of the afternoon, and she wrote them down with solemn and intense concentration. "Just remember, now," he told her in parting, "Uncle Jim never killed nobody that didn't deserve it."

I used to urge my father to tell my friends about how he got the knife blade broken off in his back, and he was always ready to oblige. It was the stuff of legend to me that he had been walking around for twenty years with the end of that blade embedded deep in the flesh, somewhere near his spine. We had an X-ray picture of it that I would dig out of the trunk and show to friends. I only afterward learned why my mother did not like the X-ray, the questions, or the story about it. The story my father told was not the true one. The truth was that he had been caught in the act of trespassing by an irate husband and the blade was a souvenir of that husband's wrath.

The old would tell ghost stories, folk tales really, that were more than half believed. They had happened, usually, to someone known by the teller's grandfather or -mother or the old man who used to live in that swamp over by Archusa Creek; terrifying tales of unexplained violence, of sudden apparitions, of people who returned from the dead, of voices in the night and whisperings in chimney corners; they frequently ended with the sentence, "And from that day to this, he has never been heard of again." One listened in fear and awe, and the flickering firelight threw fantastic patterns onto the ceiling and made all things seem possible.

Those of us who are derived from this storytelling tradition and who write are sometimes accused of exaggeration. On the contrary, the alterations we make upon the actual are more often in the direction of simplifying the truth for the sake of credibility. When I introduce the name of Mr. Raspberry into conversation, for instance, or that of Aunt Della Belcher or of a great-grandmother named Doll Flowers, my friends' sympathetic smiles tell me that they think I'm borrowing from Southern fiction in a pathetic attempt to make myself interesting. In 1959 I worked as a technical adviser on the filming of Faulkner's *Sanctuary*, and one of my responsibilities was to see that the movie had some genuine Southern flavor. I also appeared briefly in a party scene in which most of the actors gave themselves lines like "Isn't this a lovely party?," "Oh, divine," and other such imaginative remarks, but as the camera panned past me I turned to Lee Remick and said, "My sister Janice married one of the Featherstone triplets, William, Jennings, and Bryan," figuring you couldn't be more authentically Southern than that, since it was absolutely true. Alas, when Those In Authority caught my bit in the rushes, there was consternation, and the cutter had to go to a good deal of trouble to snip around me, for they found my line "terribly distracting and highly implausible."

People don't really talk to each other as they once did. At parties, at dinners, we exchange the same kind of banalities that the actors used in the party scene in the film; we ask questions out of politeness and do not bother to listen to replies. A catalogue of likes and dislikes is not conversation. It's of no more relevance than whether your sister had her breakfast eggs scrambled or sunny-side up. It's nothing more than a pretense of animation to get you through the evening. No perception has been brought into play; no insights have been revealed; no light has been thrown on anything. You know no more of the speaker when he has finished than you did when he began. People actually seem to fear that they've been impolite if they've told you anything personal; they sometimes apologize if they've slipped into honest moments. I don't give a damn about the weather; either today's, next week's, or last summer's in Venice. My face freezes at the sound of "Have you heard the one about . . . ?" And I don't care which is the best place to eat in Philadelphia. When I first came to New York, it seemed to me that I sat through dinner after dinner with partners who talked of nothing but restaurants, and I felt sadly deficient in being unable ever to remember the names of any of them. Finally I had a dream in which I met my two idols, Eleanor Roosevelt and Adlai Stevenson, and all they wanted from me was the name of a good restaurant. The best I could come up with in this nightmare was a sentence I'd heard somewhere: "They have marvelous osso buco at Sardi's on Tuesdays." I've sometimes sat and managed occasional replies to compulsive chatter that made absolutely no sense at all, a meaningless mixture of phrases picked up here and there and sprinkled about like salt on popcorn.

Even gossip is better. At least it has a subject. It has active verbs. It's almost always interesting, sometimes it contains humor, and the most uninspired of talkers can usually rise above himself to tell it fairly well.

Few people are really boring if they talk about something they are truly interested in. Lynn Fontanne, the great actress, once began a conversation with me by saying, "I'm not clever. I've never been clever, and I never say clever things, but if you're interested in the minutiae of our lives, I can tell you all about them." I *was* interested, and she did tell me, and it was fascinating. I heard all about her sewing her own dresses, about the man in Genesee Depot who baked bread, and about the chipmunks in her garden. She went on from there to describe Noel Coward's stone-cold eyes and the quarrels she'd had with him. She told about a long period during rehearsals of one of his plays when she'd stopped speaking to him, and how, when she eventually decided she'd better make it up for the good of the production, she beckoned him over at a party, raised her hand in a beautiful gesture of benediction, and said, "I forgive you." Miss Lynn didn't have to make clever remarks. She was interested in what she was saying.

When my father and his friends sat about in our yard in the evenings, the lights of their cigarettes glowing in the darkness, and talked of horses they'd known, of mistakes they'd made, of bridges that had been washed out in floods, or of painted women they'd encountered in New Orleans, they were talking about what moved them, the stuff of which their lives had been made; and their language had music in it.

As I was setting down these words, Carter came into the room, peered at the paper in the typewriter, and asked, "What are you writing about now?" I replied that I was saying that families no longer sit around and tell each other stories, and he said emphatically, "We do." Later, in the presence of Anderson, I started to tell my wife about Carter's comment, and, before I got to it, Anderson interrupted at the same point that Carter had. "We do!" he said. They are right. We do. We tell each other about experiences that befell us during the day, the funny woman we saw on the bus arguing with the driver because she wanted to go somewhere the bus didn't go to, the child who behaved badly in school, the person they saw being arrested at F. A. O. Schwarz.

My boys like to talk and they take care to tell a story well. They set the stage, they let the tension grow, they build to the climax, and then they turn loose when the point is made. If they're telling about Anderson's pet snake getting out of his cage, they describe their discovery that he was gone, Anderson's dismay, the nurse's fear (she doesn't like snakes for some reason). They tell how they checked the gerbils to see that he hadn't gotten one of their babies; how they looked under chairs, under beds, inside the bedclothes, up the chimney, and how they found him finally curled up in the crown of a sixteenth-century madonna. Or if their friend Alessandro fell off his new ten-speed bike, they describe how fast he was going, the depth of the hole in the road that caused it, the loudness of his outcry as he fell, how one went for help while the other comforted, how frightened they were, and how contemptuous they both felt for the third friend, who neither helped nor comforted but only stared, how desperately the mother ran, and how quickly Alessandro recovered.

In the old days we made our own entertainment. It was not packaged and imposed or presented, whole and entire; it did not turn us into passive spectators. We were in charge of it; it was not in charge of us. If we were interested in baseball, we got up a game with sisters filling in, or hired hands, or anyone we could persuade;

or we got together with friends and made our way to some ball-park where a game was going on. The point is that we didn't sit and watch the experts at it in six-inch-high figures on a television screen.

There is nothing inherently wrong with the existence of television or any other inventions that can bring great richness into our lives. I do not agree with those who call it a wasteland. It's a fantastic invention; it is a powerful communicator of news and information; it is difficult, today, really to maintain total ignorance of world affairs. Major events around the globe are made instantly known to us, and only the most determined can avoid exposure to some information. They get scraps of education in spite of themselves; they get it while passing through the room or while they are turning the dial to find something more sopo-rific. My children know about people, places, and things that children in previous generations might have gone to school for years and never have learned about. The important thing, I think, is that you don't let the TV set become a mechanical baby-sitter either for your children or for yourself, that you don't sit before it out of habit, absorbing nothing, mesmerized and stunned, with mouth hanging open and arms gone dead, as if you'd been hit over the head with a hammer. It should not replace activity.

It is not quite exact to say that progress is the enemy. Perhaps I mean to say that it is the by-products of progress that do us in. I think that the thing that disturbs me most about this progressive battle to overcome nature—for that is what it is: we subdue nature; we distort it; we bend it to suit our purposes—the thing that disturbs me is that with each step in which we succeed we get that one step further removed from man's natural state.

What do I mean? One enters one's front door and one touches a light switch and the dark room is instantly as bright as day. That's an improvement over what we had at my house when I was young. There's no argument there. No mother today has to say to her child, as my mother used to say to me all the time, "You're going to put your eyes out reading by that firelight." (I knew it wouldn't; it hadn't done it to Abe Lincoln, and I suspected that it might even make me President someday.) One doesn't have to come in at night, grope in the dark for a box of matches, and, finding them, look for the kerosene lamp, and, finding that, still in the dark, take off the glass globe, strike the match, light the wick, and then take it from room to room in order to light other lamps. So we agree, it's much better, much safer, much healthier, to have electric light.

But in this pushing of electric switches there is something missing that used to be there in the lighting of the lamps at home. Our way did not displace one's relationship to nature. The kerosene lamp was itself an invention intended to help overcome nature, in this case the element of darkness, and it fulfilled that purpose. When one groped in the dark looking for a lamp, one was very much aware of the existence of darkness, and in lighting the lamp, which you had yourself filled with kerosene, the wick of which you had yourself trimmed and inserted, you could feel that you were overcoming the natural dark of night by *your* own efforts; therefore you, as a man, or as a woman, had accomplished something. When you push a light switch, the impulses flow along wires installed by some electrical specialist, and the power comes from some power plant, the location of which you probably do not even know, by some process that you do not understand. It is all the work of strangers, and you fill no role in it beyond the rather abstract one of paying the bill. This is a small thing, but when it is multiplied by an army of accessories—vacuum cleaners, toasters, dishwashers, shoe polishers, toothbrushes even—the active person in charge of his own welfare somewhere gets lost. After all, you were once taught to take care of yourself, to tie your own shoes and to brush your own teeth, and at the time you learned these tasks the acquisition of the skills needed to perform them seemed like enormous victories. In the intimidating presence of all these chugging motors and whirling devices, the man tying his shoes is small potatoes indeed. Far from feeling like the Lord of the Universe, he feels as if he has become the conductor of an orchestra of mechanical aids.

Once an invention is there, of course, there's no turning back. Mankind is not going to decide not to use it. But we have been plunging recklessly on for so long that it is necessitating a complete rethinking of our attitudes about just what we need and what we don't need, a rethinking that we are only just now undertaking. We will also have to give thought not only to our own individual needs but to the needs of our neighbors as well, a concern for the collective good that we have not exactly been trained for. Our entire way of life—our advertising, our merchandising, the health of our economy—has depended upon the constant escalation of consumption. We've come to some sort of crisis where we're going to have to manage in some other way. Everybody will be forced to live with less: less space, less waste, less duplication, less obsolescence. We may find that simpler is better, that less is more.

When my father and his father before him spent their days working in the fields, planting cotton, corn, potatoes, toiling under a hot sun, feeling the sweat roll down their faces, they knew what it was for. When they came home at sundown, tired and worn-out, aching in every muscle, they knew that it was good, and why they were tired, and they were at peace within themselves. When harvest time was over, men could stand triumphantly alone in the fields and know that they faced the winter's cold with a store of grain that they had themselves coaxed from the soil. They could stand, humble under the vast vault of the heavens, and whisper thanks to a known and living God. Since they lived or died according to the mercies of the sun and rain, they could hear His voice in the thunder. They could feel, then, a kinship with nature and with nature's God; they could feel at one with those men like themselves who had also dug with their hands into the earth to find sustenance for their young. They could rejoice in their own strength, their own creation. The shape of their lives, the nature of their work, had changed little in all the centuries since the Biblical days of Abraham and Isaac with their fields and their flocks. They could see in their daily toil the fulfillment of God's commandment to Adam that all the days of his life he would earn his bread by the sweat of his brow. Even in the towns one's work had meaning. The merchant who sold the seed, the fertilizer, and the tools; the druggist who measured out the medicine; the station agent who unloaded the freight; the electrician; the plumber; the bricklayer—all knew what they did and they knew the people they did it for. The work they did had a recognizable use and place, and they could take satisfaction in that. The further we move from these roots, the less we know ourselves, the less we recognize each other. We need now, each in whatever way we can, to find the path back to a sense of the earth and of the seasons and of those cycles of birth, bloom, and death that show us man's life in miniature.

These days, most of us shuffle papers for a living. We sit in offices with people who are virtual strangers to us. We dispatch papers to other unknown people in unknown places. We sell products the value of which we do not know, and if we lose our jobs and move to a rival company, we sell its products with the same manufactured enthusiasm we exhibited before. Our jobs have titles that do not explain: the associate production supervisor of the product division. Our wives do not know what they mean. Our children do not know what they mean, and we see no definition of ourselves in them. Our work has become abstract, as remote from our lives as numbers set down on a page. We join unions and argue about wages. We go on strikes and we win raises, but we don't find pride in what we've made.

Nor have we in America been totally comfortable about our leisure time. Out of some Puritan sense of guilt, I suppose, a suspicion that it is a sin to play unless there is profit in it, we contrive to make our recreation as uncomfortable as possible. We journey great distances with hot and restless children to blister ourselves on a crowded beach, then swear and bluster at the heavy traffic coming back, and we end up wondering why we do not feel relaxed. We stand in line to get into places we do not want to be in, simply because it is something people do on their day off, and, sometimes, because our boss does it.

I was talking once with a man who had been telling me that I should play golf so that I might entice Jack Warner, then head of Warner Brothers Studios at which I was working as a screenwriter, into playing golf with me, presumably so that I might, in the camaraderie of the golf links, persuade that gentleman to promote me, raise my salary, or give me better assignments. I protested that I had no interest whatever in the game of golf, and almost as little interest in Mr. Warner as Mr. Warner would have in me in the unlikely event that he should ever become aware of my existence, a position that my friend found so outlandish that he simply could not grasp it. He himself worked night and day without joy or pleasure, plotting and scheming, because he was determined to be rich and retired at forty. I asked him what he planned to do when he got where he wanted to go. He was startled for a moment; obviously the question had never occurred to him. Then he said, "I'll play golf." He had golf on the brain. "Do you like to play golf?" I asked. He stared at me as if he despaired of ever getting any sense into my head. "No," he said, "I don't. But by God, I'll learn to like it."

I am concerned that unless we are able to find some identity for ourselves, something beyond all the numbers we are known by, beyond our position in the assembly line, something in us we can recognize and respect and live with in some degree of comfort, then we will not dare to form families, to be parents.

Without pride man is nothing, a perambulating vegetable—suspicious, resentful, negligent, and irresponsible. Without it he can have no strength, only toughness; no gentleness, only weakness; and no compassion, only self-pity. Without pride parents cannot hope to teach sons to be men, daughters women, their children adults.

In a way we have become like animals in captivity. When you remove an animal from his native habitat, his behavior is affected. Certain ones adapt, and, in time, turn into a new kind of creature. Others become disoriented. They have a set of instincts and impulses that do not apply in a protected situation. Some will refuse to eat. Some will not breed. Some will destroy or devour their young. Some lose their ability to defend themselves and, if set free again, will not remember how to find food. We are clever and we are adaptable, but there are limitations, and in the cages we have come to live in we are developing some strange aberrations.

Man has always lived with revolutions and upheavals; he has sought change and valued it, as well he might. He has, with justification, prided himself on his adaptability and his general resourcefulness, but change has come so fast lately that his talent for adapting is strained to the breaking. Future shock isn't something that's coming in the future. We are already living in it.

I know that much of what I have said has a retrogressive ring to it, and that does not please me. I do not mean to talk as if I were against advancement and inventions and technology. I do not advocate a return to an earlier and simpler time. Even if it were possible, I have no desire to do without fast airplanes and well-supplied hospitals; I enjoy much of the hustle and bustle of modern life, and the roar of cities excites me. I have become accustomed to the usefulness of frozen foods, instant coffee, and perfumed soap. Modern plumbing, air conditioning, vitamin pills, and painless dentistry I take for granted. I like drive-ins and I love to go to the movies. But progress has given us a sometimes artificial world, and we have to remind ourselves not to confuse appearance with reality. We're so determined to control our environment that I sometimes fear we'll succeed in abolishing weather. It is a world in which little that we see, touch, work with, or feel during an average day has much of anything to do with what nature made. It is hard to connect those plastic-wrapped vegetables in our freezer with anything that grew in the soil. The milk seems to have originated in a carton, and to have no connection with the friendly family cow I used to milk in the mornings before school. When she ate bitter herbs, her milk would be bitter; we would complain about that, but still, it was another link with nature.

What I want, really, is to live in a world that weighs matters carefully and counts the consequences. We've been making technological advances and our sense of self has not grown along with them. The world has been in the hands of specialists, each pushing as far forward as possible with his particular interest. One feels that they don't even check with each other; they don't compare notes, and there has been no overview. Our technology has made for much obsolescence, but, too often, what replaces that which has been discarded is no better. I want to live with people who remember where they came from, who remember the whys and hows of it, who have some idea of who they are, and a notion, at least, of where they want to go.

8

Mostly a Matter of Roots

*"Let us now praise famous men, and our fathers
that begat us."*   *—Ecclesiasticus 44:1*

Ours is a fluid society, and I thank God for it, otherwise I'd still be plowing up the red clay hills of Clarke County; but we must recognize that it is not an unmixed blessing.

Some years ago in Italy I asked a young man what he planned to be when he got out of school and he said, "I'm lucky. My father is a waiter in a coffee shop and he can get me on there." To an American that reply is unthinkable. It would not occur to us that our occupations or our station in life should be determined by those of our fathers. In this sense, we are as nearly classless a society as there has ever been. Birth and class are not major proccupations with us, and the social or economic group we are born into is not expected to dictate the shape of our lives. Even the rich among us, while they certainly start off with what we call "advantages," by no means have it made. Rarely can they coast along on inherited money for more than a generation. "Shirt-sleeves to shirtsleeves in three generations" is a description that has usually prevailed in American families. We have been proud of those of our Presidents or other heroes who have come from humble beginnings, and those citizens who've been born among the mighty have generally been subject to rather severe testing, so that the seriousness of their intent, the quality of their endurance, the basic strength of their mettle must be proven before they are accepted. The heads of our colleges or of our giant corporations may well be the sons or daughters of near-illiterate farmers; our senators may have begun life as druggists, as schoolteachers, or even as actors. Our present President of the United States once worked as a professional model. On the other hand, persons bearing illustrious names from American history can be found clerking in stores, driving taxis, or, possibly, living on welfare.

We pay a price for this fluidity, and the penalty is in the loss of those anchors in a time and place that tell us who we are. The Italian boy could follow his father into the coffee shop with some contentment, even pride. There would be for him no feeling that he had betrayed his potential. He would remain in his old community; his associates would be drawn from the children of those with whom his parents had associated; and he could rejoice in a certain continuity.

For better or worse, that is not our way. We struggle to better ourselves, and whether we succeed or not, we experience anxiety and various degrees of estrangement. We sometimes come to live with a vague sense of shame about our origins and an undefined feeling of disappointment about our accomplishments.

We have become a nation of transients. There are various estimates of how often the average American moves; some say every eight years, some say every four years; certainly among those of child-bearing age the rate is high. Almost nobody lives where he started out from, and it is difficult for parents, in such a situation, to form genuine ties to the community in which they temporarily find themselves; for children it is next to impossible. When my stepson Chris was small, he became very attached to a little girl who lived next door to a place my wife had rented for the summer. When my wife said to Chris that perhaps the girl might be his girl friend when he grew up, he said, "But how will I ever find her?" To a child the dilemma is very real. His acquaintances seem to be on conveyer belts traveling in an opposite direction.

We are trying to learn to live today without those roots that in the past afforded us the reassurance of stability, permanence, and continuity. Most of our children could not tell you the names of their grandparents. We have moved into a time when our children can say, with Napoleon's General Junot, that they are their own ancestors.

The farmhouse I lived in as a boy was the one in which my mother had been born. The house had been across the road and had been placed on logs and rolled, with the help of neighbors, to its present location, where my father had added more rooms to it. A crape myrtle bush, planted by her father about the time she was born, was also dug up and moved. When I was eighteen years old and we went to live in Meridian, I went back to the farm, dug up that bush and took it to the city. Today, nearly eighty years after it began its life, and two years after my mother's death, the flowering tree still blooms for the strangers who've gone to live in the old house on Fifth Street.

Beyond our peach orchard three generations of my mother's family lay buried. Her grandmothers Rixie Lee and Jane Anderson, both of whose first names she bore, were buried there. Fletcher Campbell, the humorless Scotsman, slept under a dark gray obelisk. Four of my mother's brothers and sisters who died in infancy were buried there, as was my sister Hazel, who died shortly before I was born. My father's notorious great-uncle, Jim Bull, was buried in the Campbell plot, for he had married my mother's aunt, Alabama Campbell (" 'Bama" for short), and on his grave thrived a large colony of giant red ants. Today my father's grave is there as well.

I knew about those people. I knew which ancestor had died in a duel, which ones fought in the Civil War, and which one avoided service; I knew which one had hewed out the benches for the church. I could wander among the graves and speculate about their lives, and, once a year, on Memorial Day, a service was held at the church, and we brought flowers for all the graves.

Eighteen miles away was my father's birthplace. It was set deep in a vast tract of virgin timber. When you arrived at my grandfather's land, the public road ended and there was an old wooden gate which had to be opened to proceed. His own road was narrow and primitive, and here and there alongside it were deep red gullies that to a child seemed as deep and dangerous as the Grand Canyon.

The original part of that house was made of logs, built a century before by my grandfather's grandfather. As the family had prospered and as its numbers had grown, new wings and porches had been added on, including the then obligatory Victorian bay-fronted room. The kitchen was a separate building at the back, attached to the main house by a covered gallery; this was to prevent the spread of flames if the kitchen caught fire, and between kitchen and house, under the roof of the gallery, was the well, so deep that, to a child peering into it, it seemed to have no bottom. The gallery, open to the air, ran through the center of the house as well; here it was called a dog run because, on cold nights, the pack of hunting dogs took refuge from the weather. Lightning rods were strung like lace all along the roof, and the house contained two pieces of furniture I coveted. One was a large dark square piano, brought from Mobile in a wagon drawn by oxen; the other was my grandfather's bed, a tall walnut affair with a headboard that went nearly to the ceiling, where it was topped off by a carved eagle.

His store, abandoned but still standing, was down the hill from his house; it straddled the Mississippi-Alabama state line so that it could house a post office serving both states. (And, presumably, so that grandchildren could, as we did, stand spraddle-legged and say, "Look at me; I've got one foot in Mississippi and the other in Alabama!") The pigeonhole letter slots were still there, and in them were ancient letters, dry and stiff with age. On the shelves, among other relics from the past, were unsold slates of the kind that schoolchildren in my father's time used for writing their lessons.

My father told me that somewhere in the garden between the house and the store a treasure was supposed to be buried, silver and gold hidden from the Yankee soldiers; that it had often been dug for, but never found. I believed him then and would like to believe him now, had I not since then heard the same story about so many other gardens in the South, and had I any reason to believe that any branch of the Northern army saw fit to venture into that remote section of the country.

Farther into the forest, beyond the ruins of the grist mill, and reached only by tracing the almost obliterated evidence of an old wagon road, was the family graveyard, already at that time unused for at least a generation.

I went there once, in a large group called together by a relative named Kanzadie Walker (she had been a Wyatt) for the purpose of erecting a tombstone on somebody's grave. I believe you could then write away somewhere and get a free tombstone for veterans of the Civil War and Kanzadie had done that for long-dead Uncle Rob Somebody—whether Cooper, Wyatt, Flowers, Bull, or Boykin, I do not remember. We made the journey to Grandpa's in Lee Dearman's school bus, a festive load of us, and at Grandpa's we had to leave the bus and continue the remaining couple of miles on foot with several brawny youths taking turns at stumbling along bearing the marble tombstone horizontally between them, while I, with Dwayne, Namon, Naomi, and others of my age, ran, in our excitement, ahead of the party and then back again, making elongated circles like impatient puppies. ("Don't get close to that Dwayne, Namon, and Naomi," my mother had admonished me that morning. "Half that family's had TB and it's catching.")

Chattering and laughing, our group invaded the deep integrity of the woods like an intruding army of alien creatures, the noise of our approach preceding us in sharp, crackling waves, unsettling the summer calm, setting off a squawking of blue jays, a cawing of crows, a disturbance of decades of peace. Kanzadie, she of the monumental and complacent bulk, maintained the lead; she was the general, the mover, the one who had caused the event to take place, and, along the way, she exercised her familiarity with the dead. "Aunt Maggie went in the 'flu epidemic of '97,' and it was consumption that took Aunt Jessie," and "Grandpa Bull was away back in them swamps ahunting—you know how he loved to hunt —when he fell dead and it took them four days to find him."

We came upon the cemetery unexpectedly and without warning. Suddenly, in the deep shadows of the tall trees and from the dense growth of bushes, there emerged directly in our path a white marble angel with wings outspread almost as if in protest. The spaces of its eyes were dark growths of fungus; on its shoulders and along the backs of its wings was an accumulation of years of fallen pine straw, and dead and rotting leaves. Spiders nested in the open mouth, and from its streaked and time-stained whiteness, it seemed to utter a soundless cry of outrage. Unseen and unsung, for seasons without number, it had stood its silent sentinel, through heat and cold, disdaining rain and lightning and thunder, and, after all this time, it seemed no more native to the place—it bore no more relation to the spirits of those people of a raw and unschooled race whose graves it guarded—than it did all those years ago when some ancestor—even Kanzadie did not know who—had had it hauled here, like the piano, from some city where ships came and went. One wondered how it had come about; one wondered by what impulse toward grandiosity, by what expression of hopeful prosperity, by what sense of dynastic necessity, by what sudden surge of religious feeling, or by what unlikely gesture toward beauty, our unknown progenitor had been propelled into the transaction of purchase by which this exotic product of a distant land, carved into being by foreign hands, came to be transported here to last out its eternity in endless exile.

Behind and around it the wilderness had taken over; tangles of briars, huckleberry, ferns, and masses of undergrowth completely hid the rusty iron fence that had once enclosed the lot, the fence that still stood but only to crumble at the touch.

Kanzadie took charge and issued orders. We had come armed with hoes, rakes, axes, and other implements for clearing land, and, while the privileged young among us climbed and played about, the men set to work. There was disagreement about where some graves were, but any question was settled by Kanzadie, and it was right that it should be so for she was an authority on burials.

"Here's Great-Grandma Boykin," she would say of a gray moss-covered stone, the carving on which was no longer decipherable, and "I remember Aunt Bett was put next to her and Cousin Willis was put right next to Aunt Bett," and "No, Emmett, you're wrong. That couldn't be where Uncle Rob is, because that's where they buried that little chap of Caroline's. I remember it was right down from Grandpa's feet. Used to be a wooden cross over it that Granddaddy Flowers made," and "Just over there, where that big oak is now, that's where they buried that little nigra of Uncle Press's that drowned at the grist mill."

My father showed me where his Great-Grandfather Beryl Boykin was buried. I asked to see his grave, because that grandfather had been murdered, knocked in the head with a singletree by a rebellious slave, who was then tied to a tree and burned, allegedly by the other slaves.

Papa, less impressed by Kanzadie's encyclopedic recall than I was, was certain that we'd placed the new Confederate tombstone over quite the wrong person (over Caroline's baby, actually), but he didn't think it was worth quarreling over. "Never mind," he said to me, when I worried about it, "it made Kanzadie happy, and it don't make a damned bit of difference to Uncle Rob."

Since the subject at hand is the question of roots, the need for roots, the desirability of having roots, and our alarm at the present lack of them, and since I have just devoted a number of pages to a discussion of graveyards (on the questionable grounds, perhaps, that you can't be more firmly rooted than that), and, further, since I have, in the progress of this narrative, told of a dismaying number of calamitous ends (with still more to come), presenting what is undoubtedly an inaccurate and unfair portrait of my relatives as a clan no member of which ever died peacefully in his bed, I must admit that the perceptive reader may, at this point, with justification, find himself making the observation, "If these are roots, I will happily live without them!"

In defense of my kin, I submit that they have, no matter what I've implied elsewhere, generally lived the peaceful, law-abiding lives of decent citizens, happy in comfortable obscurity, and they will not now appreciate my thus holding up their more colorful members for public appraisal.

In defense of my proposition that roots in the past are a precious thing, I can only say that it is not at all a matter of having *splendid* roots, with illustrious and distinguished forebears decorating the pages of history. The important thing about roots, really, is not how enviable they are, but that they are there at all. The real difference, to me, and to you, is in feeling related. And related is what we don't feel much of these days—not to our neighbors, not to our fathers, not to our brothers, not to our children, not to our past, not to our present, and, God help us, not to our future.

For me, as a child moving among those graves, running my

curious fingers along those monuments to my past, there was nothing morbid or disturbing in seeing my ancestors laid out in rows according to their generations. Through it I came to know that I belonged to a long line of people—once alive, human, and vulnerable—a chain of humanity that extended back to the beginning of time. It enlarged one's perspective beyond the here and now. It wasn't simply that one was told, or that one read history books. One saw it and felt it in one's bones; I was a member of that hardy race that had struggled and fought and laughed and cried all along the centuries; I was one with those people who had followed Moses out of Egypt, who had climbed the Alps with Hannibal, who had wrestled the Magna Carta from old King John, who had gone to battle with Cromwell's armies, and who had crossed a perilous ocean in search of life and liberty and little patches of dirt they could call their own.

And there, among the Cape jasmine and the crape myrtle, rested those of my forebears who had picked their way through primeval swamps and traveled uncharted miles along undiscovered rivers until they settled on these acres in Mississippi and Alabama. Out of their courage and strength and hope and dignity, or perhaps simply out of their dire necessity, they had ventured with frail feet into the threat of unknown forests, to wrest a living out of an alien land and people a nation out of their pain and sweat and sorrow.

A child could stand, as I stood, with his bare feet digging into the sand of their graves and know that their toil and their despair, their trials and their triumphs, were forever a part of him, just as their dust and their bones were forever a part of the land.

I could see that the world did not begin with me. I could see that I was a part of all that went before, and they, those vanished thousands, are forever a part of what I am and of what I shall be.

It is important for a child to know that. The world does not begin nor end with him, and in between his being born and his dying, he has a link to forge. He has a challenge, a chance, and a responsibility.

If we know that, we can feel related to the past—we can feel ourselves derived from it, and a participant in it, without its being tied only to the faded names or the fading portraits of our grandfathers.

And we must encourage ourselves to do so. I have many spiritual ancestors toward whom I feel infinitely more drawn than I do toward the late Beryl Boykin. Thomas Jefferson, for one. I can read about his life and study his words, and I can recognize something there with which I identify; in his thoughts, his style, and his aspirations there is something to which I feel related, that I feel derived from, and that I can, in my own small way, seek to emulate.

In the world in which we now find ourselves, in which there are few family tombstones, few family stories, few family trees, and few family ties, we will have to do that—make all the world's history into our family history. The Jewish people have in times past had a religion and an ethnic system that kept alive the race's history, and, along with that, the individual's sense of sharing a common heritage. My children know something of their ancestors, but I want them also to feel that all the past is a part of their inheritance, and all the people in that past. Once Anderson was leaving the Museum of Natural History in New York with his class and the teacher pointed to the gigantic equestrian statue of Theodore Roosevelt outside and asked if anyone knew who he was. Now my son had seen statues of some of his ancestors. There is a rather imposing one of Commodore Cornelius Vanderbilt, his great-great-great-grandfather, at Grand Central Station, and another at Vanderbilt University in Nashville; at home we have a bronze bust of Reginald Vanderbilt, my wife's father, so Anderson had, I suppose, gotten an impression either that when grandfathers die they turn into statues or that all statues are grandfa-

1901. Grandpa Cooper was one of nature's aristocrats. He followed no lights but his own and left a string of illegitimate children to prove it. On his deathbed in his eighty-fourth year he kept shouting that if they'd bring a woman to his bed he'd have no need of dying.

Cousin Emma Boykin painted angels on her ceiling and gave each of them her own face. She also wrote a song called "Mizpah." Her talents were relentless but not complicated by great skill.

Uncle Jim Bull fought at Chickamauga and never shook off the habit of killing. He once shot a man for cussing in front of womenfolks, but, according to my father, he never killed anybody who didn't deserve it.

My mother's side was more moral. Here are her grandparents, Martha Jane and Ben Anderson, at the Pleasant Grove Baptist Church, which he helped build. Still, we were not to speak to him, for he and my father got into a dispute over the boundary line between their properties.

Her other grandmother, Rixie Lee, was gay and high-spirited but married to a sour Scotsman named Fletcher Campbell, a schoolmaster who disapproved of learning, leading, as it did, to a frivolous view of life.

My mother (seated) at nine. Her face already reflected that inner serenity she was never to lose. She would need it for the years with my father.

Papa at seventeen. The man I remember was a creature of charm, magnetism, tyranny, and madness. This photograph reminds me of something else: his sad, hooded eyes, often turned inward toward remembered pain.

The first time my father saw my mother, he announced that he would marry her as soon as she was old enough. He went to Panama, waited two years, then came back and married her in 1910. She was fourteen. He was twenty-two.

Another of my children's distinguished ancestors (from their mother's family, of course; all the famous ones are hers) is Judson Kilpatrick, the youngest of Lincoln's generals. To my sons the Confederates are "Daddy's side" and the Union is "Mommy's side," reducing that conflict to the status of a domestic spat.

This statue of Commodore Cornelius Vanderbilt, my wife's great-great-grandfather, stands at Grand Central Station, and there's another at Vanderbilt University; so my son Anderson got the idea that grandfathers, when they die, turn into statues.

"You listen to me, boy, and I'll make you the youngest Goddamned governor Mississippi ever had!" Papa said. He was determined to mold me into a young Theodore G. Bilbo, but I saw myself as more of an Ashley Wilkes type, and somehow I'd picked up a devotion to the social concerns of Mrs. Roosevelt that played hell with Papa's molding.

Miss Onie Acklin's fifth-grade class at Cedar Creek School. My aunt commented, "Wouldn't you know you'd be the one who sat with his legs different from the others?" I notice that I was also the one who troubled to comb his hair.

We kept a large selection of uniforms, and choosing costumes was the first things chums did on arrival, but Carter was pained by others' carelessness about mixing historical periods. "Crusaders fighting Romans!"

Christmas card photograph, 1971. The tall fellow with the facial hair is Chris Stokowski, my stepson.

On the bluffs above the Mississippi River at Natchez, September, 1974. The reason my sons, who are joyous persons, are rarely smiling in my photographs is that they are tired of waiting for me to focus. They have beautiful smiles, as can be seen in the photograph on the book jacket taken by Cris Alexander, who has good eyesight and focuses quickly.

thers, for when the teacher asked that question, his hand shot up. "I tink it's my grandfadder," he said.

Well, Theodore Roosevelt isn't his grandfather, and yet, in another sense, he is. He is everybody's grandparent, and so are George Washington, Abraham Lincoln, Franklin D. Roosevelt, the Wright Brothers, Thomas Edison, Madame Curie, and Sigmund Freud. We are descended from them as surely as we are descended from all those strangers whose genes we bear. What they were and what they did are a part of what we are and what we do. We can even choose our own. When he was in the first grade, Anderson came home and said he was reading a book about Helen Keller and liked it so much he wanted us to buy him a copy of it. He talked about her, asked about her, tried to imagine what it would be like to be blind and deaf, and something in him responded to her strength and courage and determination; and, at that tender age, whatever it was in her life that he responded to—that became a part of his own life.

We do not have to hold such models up to our children as marble heroes of shining perfection. For one thing, we can't get away with it; those of my generation may have believed old Parson Weems's tale of George Washington chopping down a cherry tree and saying, "I cannot tell a lie," but our children are just as likely to know that he also padded his expense account. Perfection is not the issue. Humanity is. Flawed persons are recognizable because we learn very early on that we ourselves are flawed. Real grandfathers aren't perfect either, any more than fathers are, and accepting that lack of perfection in Dad, Gramps, and the Father of Our Country is a part of that coming to terms with our own nature, of accepting our own humanness, that each of us has to do. My children have a sword that belonged to another ancestor of theirs (on their mother's side, of course; the famous ones are all on her side). He was General Judson Kilpatrick, the youngest of Lincoln's generals. (They refer to the Union Army as "Mummy's side," while the Confederates are "Daddy's side," reducing that calamitous conflict to the status of a domestic spat.) They are proud of that sword, intrigued to think that he might actually have wielded it in battle, and they like to show their friends a photograph of the short and bearded warrior, but I'm certain that they have no illusions that he was lacking in the usual frailties or that he never made disastrous mistakes or never lost a battle through his own misjudgment. Perfection is no longer required of those we admire or are proud of, and that's fine. It's more honest, more acceptable. Humanity in a person is more desirable than perfection, and, anyway, any Southern schoolchild can tell you that the only truly perfect man who ever lived was Robert E. Lee.

I am sometimes asked if my children are aware of the part their mother's family has played in American social history, as if there were some singular circumstance in being a Vanderbilt that required special handling in telling one's children about it, and I am reminded of Sarah Churchill's reply when asked what it was like to be the daughter of Sir Winston and Lady Churchill. "It was like having a father and a mother," she said.

The answer is, of course, that they do know and it seems no more novel or particular to them than it would if the names were of a more commonplace variety, and no more tact or discretion is required in relating their stories than there is in talking about my own less glamorous ancestors. As Carter is fascinated by architecture and the preserving of landmarks, his principal interest in Vanderbilt history has to do with the houses. He likes the Breakers at Newport better than Marble House or the one at Hyde Park; he wonders why Bergdorf Goodman, instead of tearing down my wife's grandmother's Victorian mansion that covered the block between Fifty-seventh and Fifty-eighth Streets, couldn't have left it standing and simply set up shop in the house and, in doing so, preserved it for posterity. He is curious about what sort of persons built the houses, particularly his favorite,

Biltmore, at Asheville, North Carolina, and he is fascinated by the fact that that estate had its own railroad and that the hundreds of acres of ground were laid out by Frederick Law Olmsted, who designed Central Park. A few seasons back television's *Masterpiece Theatre* presented an excellent dramatic series based on the life of John Churchill, the first Duke of Marlborough, and his ambitious Duchess. We followed it with avid interest and, with his love of things military, Carter was delighted to discover that the present Duke of Marlborough is his relative through the marriage of Consuelo Vanderbilt to the ninth Duke. When his interest is aroused, he follows through, seeking more information about the subject, and we help out. Consuelo, later Madame Balsan, had written a book, *The Glitter and the Gold,* and in it are pictures of Consuelo at Blenheim, the enormous palace built for the Iron Duke by Queen Anne and a grateful nation and named for his most celebrated battle; pictures of her in velvet and ermine as a canopy bearer to Queen Alexandra at the coronation of King Edward VII in 1902; and others of equal interest. We talked about the marriage itself, which was a most unhappy one, arranged out of Mrs. Vanderbilt's intense social ambition, and on the Duke's part, out of his need for cash.

Both boys are interested in Egyptian pyramids and other relics of that ancient civilization, and they like the idea that it was their great-great-grandfather, William Henry Vanderbilt, who brought to New York and had set up in Central Park the Egyptian obelisk called Cleopatra's Needle, around the base of which they have often played. Because the personalities in family histories intrigue me, I have told them stories about the old Commodore, some favorable, some not so favorable. They loved the plan that he submitted to Abraham Lincoln (never put into effect) that he should personally load up one of his ships with bales of cotton, set it afire, and ram the dreaded iron ship, the *Merrimac.* When we watched another television series on American history, Vanderbilts were discussed in connection with great American fortunes, robber barons, and lavish living, and we talked of it as of any other matter about which one need feel neither shame nor pride. I am sure that my children understand that any family, whether the name is Vanderbilt, Cooper, Smith, or Jones, will include among its members some persons of fine character, some of less, some who contribute and some who are useless, and I know that their sense of their own worth will not depend upon the fame or lack of it among their forebears.

If the children of the famous have to cope with a special circumstance, it is derived chiefly from the way others look at them, and how they cope with it depends largely upon how their parents cope with it. As children they soon discover that certain attentions are paid them; the parents' fame may cause them to be treated with deference in some situations and with distrust in others. Particular demands may be made for which they are not prepared or with which they are not comfortable. There are people who will express certain expectations or make certain comparisons concerning the children of the famous, expectations and comparisons that can be puzzling to the child. Reflected glory is a tricky thing; the child may enjoy the special status conferred upon him, but, at the same time, find it disturbing because it has nothing to do with what he is or what he has done.

My sons and some of their friends got into a dispute in the playground with another group of boys that included the son of a famous government figure whose name is as well known as any name in America, and that little boy drew himself up and demanded, "Do you know who I am?" as if that clinched the argument. My boys laughed about that because they do know who he is; famous surname or not, who he is is a little boy who, like any other little boy, sometimes gets into arguments. It is to be hoped, for his own good, that he will soon find out that that is, in fact, who he is. If the father is infatuated with the prerogatives of his own fame, it will be hard for the boy to feel any other way, and one day he'll come face to face with the chilling fact that it is not his family name that counts. Fame is heady stuff for anybody and it has its perils for those whose talent or work has earned it, but for those who shimmer in somebody else's spotlight it is truly dangerous. Reality gets pretty distorted in that unnatural glare, and one's perspective is as hard to maintain as one's balance.

We have often heard it said that talent skips a generation, which means, if it means anything, that grandchildren of great men more often achieve greatness for themselves than do the children. It is easy enough to find examples to illustrate that proposition; Randolph Churchill, for instance, whose talents and abilities were perhaps not fully realized because he labored under the overwhelming shadow of the gigantic symbol and towering personality of the great Winston; Randolph's son, the present Winston, seems to suffer from no such inhibitions. One can also, of course, find some examples of distinguished sons following in the steps of distinguished fathers; in the Wyeth family three generations have, in N. C., Andrew, and Jamie Wyeth, produced three major painters, but in this case it would seem that fathers and sons have been very close, very encouraging and supportive of each other's efforts. Presumably there has been no sense of rivalry or fear of replacement on the elders' parts, and fathers have inspired rather than paralyzed their sons' ambitions. Nor have the fathers been too busy or too preoccupied with their own careers and fame to take an interest in the younger men's development.

There is likely, though, to be a psychological truth in this business of skipping a generation. Thinking of it on a fairly modest, small-town scale, I know of a man whose father was president of the local bank, respected and responsible. The son suffered by comparison, and as long as his father was alive, he seemed bent chiefly on making a name for himself as the family disgrace, drinking, wenching, getting into scrapes, and dedicating himself to general hell-raising, but the minute his father died, he, like Prince Hal when he became Henry V, immediately reformed himself, took over management of the bank, and became a model citizen. Sometimes a son is not able to make that transition, or does not have the opportunity; some fathers live so long nowadays that Junior doesn't get his chance at the family business until he himself is of an advanced age; like Edward VII, who was disapproved of and cruelly isolated by Queen Victoria, they spend their lives in waiting. If the father's accomplishments are great and widely noted, the son can be made to feel very early on that he can't possibly surpass Dad's splendid record; if the father is a very strong or dominating character, the son may feel threatened if he even tries, and be defeated before he sets one foot out into the world. He may choose to apply himself in an entirely different field of endeavor to avoid comparison. If your father was a superstar like General MacArthur or General Eisenhower, you might be well advised to change your name and study chicken farming or medical research—anything but the military. On the other hand, if the general was your grandfather, the comparison is far enough removed, and the glamour of the elder's career is far enough into the past, that it can serve as a spur and an inspiration. The distance of removal can become a benign influence instead of an imminent danger.

Lately I've been reading a biography of William Faulkner. He is a personal idol; it is not only that I think he is the greatest of American novelists, but also that I feel a very personal identification with his writing. For many years, my admiration for his work inhibited my own impulses toward writing; I felt that the world I knew about had already been dealt with in Faulkner's books, and that with a mastery that I could not challenge. This was not helped by the fact that Faulkner himself looked very much like my father.

Because he had a high-spirited Great-Aunt 'Bama, of whom he once said, "When she dies, either she or God has got to leave Heaven, because both of 'em can't be boss," I have hesitated to set down much about my own Great-Aunt 'Bama. My Aunt 'Bama, after the death of Uncle Jim Bull, seemed to find a surprising number of husbands, and after her death I learned that, because she received some pension that required a permanent state of widowhood, she had never legally married any of them.

Faulkner, too, had one of these extraordinary grandfathers whose life and work were undoubtedly a tremendous influence upon the groping youth, and a colorless father whose own life was of no particular note. Colonel W. C. Falkner (the family's original spelling) was a dashing and heroic figure; lawyer, soldier, and founder of a railroad; he was responsible, in those rough Mississippi days, for the deaths of several men, and was himself shot down in the public square just after winning election to the state legislature, all of which is the stuff of which romantic Southern family legends are made, and fine material for the mind of an embryo novelist, who, in the second grade, was already saying, "I'm going to write books like my granddaddy." The old man also wrote novels, one of which, *The White Rose of Memphis*, was popular and celebrated. Now a son with literary leanings might have been intimidated by such flamboyance in a parent, but by the time young William came along the colonel was a frockcoated statue on a twelve-foot pedestal in the cemetery at Ripley, Mississippi, a statue, incidentally, that Colonel Falkner, with his eye on posterity, had commissioned and paid for well in advance of his untimely demise.

While we are in this general area of inquiry, we might pay some brief attention to certain fascinating theories about the creation of great men. It seems that the ideal situation for producing what we sometimes call overachievers is something like this: If he is male (I don't know quite how the theories apply to females), he should be born into a family with a strong, intelligent, and ambitious mother, and a father whose own accomplishments can be readily surpassed. If such a mother transfers her expectations from the father to the son and, by her devotion and faith, inspires him to feel that he can accomplish monumental things, he has a good chance, all other things being equal, to make his mark in the world. Franklin D. Roosevelt is a good example; his father was elderly and ailing, and his mother young, devoted, and as determined a character as ever was. She decided quite early on that her son was destined for greatness and preserved his baby clothes, carefully labeled, as if she knew they would someday repose in the glass cases of a museum. The stepmother of Abraham Lincoln insisted that he be allowed to study the books he loved and attend school as long as possible, over the objections of his unimaginative father, who needed another hand at the plow. There are other examples not so happy: Hitler for one, Napoleon for another.

A parent should take care that his appreciation of his child is not based upon externals; the child must not be made to feel that his acceptance and worth in his parents' eyes depend upon material accomplishments, upon the figure he cuts in the world. A child, like the rest of us, must be made to feel that he's entitled to the space he occupies; he is worthy of the skin he stands up in. He should feel his personal qualities count for more than the high marks he gets in school or for the fact that he's captain of the football team, and if the father's own self-esteem is based upon how far he's traveled in his profession, how well he's done in the competitions, then the son may well turn away from him in dismay. Better a self-respecting mediocrity for a parent than a self-despising tycoon. Children are severe moralists, and, whether they are aware of it or not, they are hoping to find in their parents those moral qualities they can admire, moral qualities that are not necessarily those exact virtues that have been responsible for the parents' worldly success. We have all known children of such successful men who have reacted by rejecting any form of success for themselves.

And, in this matter of setting goals for our children, care must be exercised. It is good to have goals and ambitions, but demands are a dangerous thing. For those strong, intelligent, and ambitious mothers (or for similar fathers) who might wish to follow this method for producing overachievers, a note of caution should be sounded. It is not a course to be recommended as a deliberate technique. Overachievers are not necessarily among the happiest of folk. For those who are driven, obsessed, insatiable, there is little contentment in victory. For those whose work is a labor of love, yes; for those who take pleasure in the doing of the thing they do, fine; but one feels sorry for those who drive on and on with little sense of what all the effort is for.

And the wise parent doesn't want to saddle his child with his own unrealized ambition. Unrealistic goals can be set that way. One can burden him with one's excessive expectations or drive him into a terrible sense of failure, to despair, defeat, and self-destruction.

We should resolve, then, that a child's sense of roots will not be dependent upon his family's name or history, or upon that family's excessive ambition for him, but upon some sense of relatedness to the world and to the realization of the place he himself wants to fill in it. We are not finished with that discussion, but before we go further into it there is another matter that must be disposed of. A few words must be said about the relationship between roots in a particular place and the principle of ethnocentrism.

I am not fond of the principle of ethnocentrism; it gave me a lot of trouble when I was young. What it means, roughly, is: *Mine is better than yours;* my team, my group, my country, my God, my dog—whatever; it's all better than yours. I didn't like that principle then and I haven't grown to like it since, and the reason for bringing it up is that it has something to do with our roots in a particular place.

"My country, right or wrong," they used to tell us in school, and that seemed as immoral to me then as it seems immoral to me now. Suppose your country is Germany under Hitler—then are you to line the streets shouting hosannahs without a thought for morality? Sometimes there are higher loyalties. There are times when principles of right or wrong are more important than the call of country, county, or clan. G. K. Chesterton once wrote that to say "My country, right or wrong" was like saying "My mother, drunk or sober."

Mr. Arthur Griffin, in the Sunday prayers which I found most edifying, used to thank God fervently for allowing him to be born in the community of Pleasant Grove. He was always thanking God for that, and for making him a Christian and, especially, a Baptist. Later, in Quitman (a town, at that time, of some fifteen hundred souls), I heard others thank God for setting them down in that place. Now, I liked Pleasant Grove and I liked Quitman; I loved the soil, the trees, the houses, the people, and the blue sky that hung over all, but those prayers bothered me. I read a great deal and a part of that reading had to do with places I longed to see: New Orleans, Atlanta, Washington, New York, London, Paris, and Rome. Furthermore, much as I loved Pleasant Grove, and devout and deserving though some of its inhabitants were, it lacked one thing I judged indispensable for my true happiness in this world—a movie theatre. My own prayers at that time were more likely to mention some hastening of the day when I could live in some possible proximity to a picture palace, when I could stop reading about movies and start seeing them, for I was an ardent film fan, and, alas, got to go only when I went home from school with some chum who lived in Quitman. I had, in that way, managed to see Laurence Olivier in both *Rebecca* and *That Hamilton Woman*, and from then on my Uncle Hal was no longer the hero I modeled myself after. I wanted to be like Laurence Olivier (listen, I still want to be like Laurence Olivier) or Leslie Howard. When *Gone With the Wind* came, I hitchhiked to town (a black man gave me a ride on a log truck) to see it. I must have been the only twelve-year-old boy in the whole state who sat through *Gone With the Wind* thinking it was a story about this nice man named Ashley Wilkes.

Still, one likes what one knows, and so most of us felt that we were blessed in living in the community we had been born into. We had ties there and we were suspicious of the dark doings that we heard were rampant in less enlightened places. The principle of ethnocentrism doubtless has its historic purpose. If you're firmly rooted in one place, there's no point in telling yourself that elsewhere is better, a principle which had its beginning long ago, when small groups had to cling together for protection and survival. It was a source of solidarity for the clan. Many tribes, in ancient times and in primitive areas today, have had a name for their group meaning "man" or "human"; all others were nonmen or nonhuman. In simple societies, after all, any outsider is a potential threat, and it is necessary that those in this family, or this valley, or that desert tribe (if we go back to Biblical times) stick together, stand up for each other, and, if need be, join together to wipe out those neighbors who practice a different brand of commerce, or have different looks, manners, customs, allegiances, and gods.

Carter Cooper was for a time very interested in Bible stories, and one night when I was reading a story in which God instructed the Hebrews to destroy the Canaanites or some other ungodly neighboring people, down to the last goat, sheep, and ass, a look of anger came over Carter's face; he reached over and closed the book with righteous decision. "And He's supposed to be such a nice Person!" he said. He was right, of course; it's no way for a God that Carter and I would approve of to be behaving, and yet

He was exactly the kind of God the Jews or anybody else had to have if they were to endure very long in that warring culture. Carter and I are products of a humanistic civilization, but it is only in the past five hundred years or so that we have begun to dismantle those authoritarian structures designed to ensure survival. When Protestantism began, with its drive toward individual responsibility for individual determination, the old powers of the absolutes, whether Gods, Popes, Kings, or Senates, would start to be undermined. You tell a man that he can read and interpret the Scriptures for himself, that he must, in the end, be the author of his own fate, that he is called upon to bypass priests and divine authorities to form his own direct relationship to God, and you've got a man on your hands who will follow that assumption to its logical conclusion. It may take centuries—it did take centuries—but we have gradually enlarged our vision to look beyond the needs, the institutions, and the pressures of our villages, our states, even of our nations, to form our own opinions, and direct our loyalties toward those principles we ourselves have chosen; and when there is a fundamental conflict, there are those who will not long let the tribe speak for them.

The dark side of ethnocentrism is that it is limiting; when it is most intense, one lives with blinders on; it compounds suspicion, fear, envy, and denial. Whatever evidence refutes the proposition that mine is best must be denied. To cling to this, one has to lie to oneself. It rejects without inspecting. What is different becomes automatically bad. Anybody of another color or religion or persuasion, anything "other," is an enemy to be destroyed lest it contaminate the purity of one's own group. Ethnocentrism enables a people to close their eyes to injustice, inequality, persecution, and exploitation. It is in opposition to the movement of history.

And so, in the thirties, we grew up in that little farming community where life and outlook had changed little in two hundred years, and the more inquiring minds among us began to study, to learn, to read books, and to think about what we read. We learned that other people in other places held other opinions and exercised other options. We found that the world is a place of extraordinary diversity and that in that diversity is great beauty. We would come to long for greener pastures and for more fruitful fields; we would widen the range of our visions and the scope of our possibilities. But in moving away from the land and the life that had made us, we were not rejecting, condemning, or abandoning the beauty, sweetness, or validity of the place or its people; we committed no disloyalty to its deeper principles or to its human concerns. We were, instead, seeking a more universal constituency; we were widening our embrace; we were pushing beyond those limitations of perspective that we had been born to, and, one hopes, following after higher principles.

I have said that in these days of diminishing family associations we must, in the absence of flesh-and-blood kin, extend our families out once again to make all history our family history, to take all those we know and love into the circle of our family's reach; just so we must take all the world, or whatever portion of it we can, into our family's grasp. Our loyalties may have been to our neighborhood. Our children's loyalties will be to all mankind. The world *is* their neighborhood. If ever it was possible that continents, nations, states, or men could exist as islands unto themselves, it is certainly no longer thinkable. Anything that happens anywhere affects us all. The tree that falls today in Pakistan echoes tomorrow across our land. Trouble cannot be isolated. Not war, not famine, not poverty, nor disaster, nor civil strife. We are already one world, and the people in it will very soon have to live together as a community if they are to live at all. Our children can understand this better than we can. Indeed, they accept it. Today's child knows and cares more about his twin on the other side of the globe than his grandfather knew about his neighbor

in the next county, and he can more readily look beyond those
differences in custom, religion, and language that separate us, to
see the more basic and universal things we have in common. And,
before we know it, the world will be theirs.

I have been talking about my youthful involvement with a
particular time, place, and people, but even as I was finding an
identity for myself at that time, in that place, and with those
people, a parallel process was also at work. To know the particular
and come to terms with it, to live in harmony with it, frees you
to move on to the general; it extends itself toward the universal.
As soon as I began to read, a fantastic and limitless world was
opened, and nothing in it was foreign to me. I discovered that my
relationships with those around me, my daydreams, my perplexities, my embryonic conclusions, my sensitivities, my sensibilities,
had all been known, felt, and expressed elsewhere and by other
persons. A thought I had been groping for, pecking my way
through the fog of my mind and trying to form, I would find
clearly and forcefully set down in the words of some Greek play-
wright some 2,500 years before. I discovered there that long
before me sons felt rage toward their fathers, men quarreled with
their gods, races struggled toward some concept of nobility,
honor, and heroism. A phrase of Shakespeare's could stick in my
mind and run through it over and over like a needle stuck on a
broken record. "Life's but a walking shadow, a poor player that
struts and frets his hour upon the stage, and then is heard no
more. It is a tale told by an idiot, full of sound and fury. . . ."
Drunk with the power and glory of such words, I would roll them
luxuriously around in my mouth, and, safe in the privacy of the
woods, hurl them out against the stolid disregard of the oaks and
pines and the quivering dogwood trees. "O full of scorpions is my
mind, dear wife," I would yell in my soprano voice, and "Now is
the winter of our discontent made glorious summer . . . ," and no
one would know, only me and the scampering gray lizard with his

unblinking eyes, and the spirit of that man who shaped the words hundreds of years before, when old Queen Elizabeth ruled my people.

I would never be alone in this universe.

Rooted though I was in the land that had belonged to my grandfathers, I learned that I had other roots, that they could grow to extend themselves around the globe, and backward and forward in time. My roots were in humanity; my relatives were all mankind; my home would be the world; and my time would be all the ages.

That's what we have to do now, all of us.

Sociologists talk a great deal these days about the disappearance of the extended family consisting of aunts, uncles, cousins, and grandparents, and the prevalence of what is called the nuclear family, an airtight unit of one, two, three, or four persons; parents (or one parent) and child or children without outside kin or antecedents, lacking the leavening influence and intervention of those other relations and generations. One reads with interest and admiration of those clans who, like the Kennedys, maintain some strong lines of communication and contact, who engage in some shared endeavor, and who assume some responsibilities toward one another and toward each other's children.

Dr. Erika Padan Freeman, psychoanalyst and professor of social psychiatry at Sarah Lawrence College in New York, notes with particular regret the absence of grandmothers. In many cases in the past where children had suffered from all the negative aspects of parenthood—abuse, neglect, hostility, or indifference —that would normally have turned the offspring into criminals at worst or neurotics at best, in those cases when that sad result had not occurred there was found in the background a grand- mother who had loved without reservation and whose support and respect had been a healing force. The absence of grandmothers today comes about for several reasons, the first being the problem of proximity; too often those grandmothers who would wish to be baking cookies for their children's children, and those grandfathers who would be taking them fishing or telling them tales of their own boyhood, live too far away to play any useful role in forming their lives. Another reason is that we aren't getting old as fast as we once did. People used to settle into such roles soon after forty. Now, at that age, we're just getting started. Better health conditions and having fewer babies have kept us much younger and more active in our middle years. We have thriving careers and sometimes even begin new ones as our children grow up and move away, when at the same chronological age many of our ancestors were old in health, vitality, and life expectancy.

The child of the nuclear family, in seeking someone to emulate, gets little by way of example except the two parents he was born to, if, indeed, he is able to hold onto both of them for very long, which is by no means always the case now that one-parent homes are far from being a rarity. Oh, maybe there are a few friends of the parents who drop in and whom the younger child may be instructed to call "uncle" or "aunt," and who gaze at him briefly and perhaps inquire politely about his age or grade in school before they move on to the den for drinks; or a real blood relative whose existence has not previously been mentioned, whose coming is labeled a nuisance and the exact degree of whose kinship has almost been forgotten, may show up from time to time; but the real feeling of "blood of my blood, bone of my bone" is not there. The child sees nothing to connect with himself.

When I saw things in my father that disturbed me and of which I disapproved, I could turn to my Uncle Walter, who seemed to me to be gently and quietly strong. When I was sixteen or seventeen and struggling for some sense of myself as an adult, and of the supportive relationship toward others that being an adult entails, I had the good fortune (or the good sense) to pick a girl friend with a father who by example taught me a great deal about what a husband and father could be. His name was Eben Watkins and he lived in New Orleans. His enthusiasm about the world was contagious and he had an unabashed love for his family that swept you along with it. On Sundays after church, Mr. and Mrs. Watkins, Alice, her brother, and I, and usually a sister or brother of my own as well, would pile into his car and go somewhere, a picnic on the levee, a trip to the bayous, or a visit to some Italian ice cream place in the French Quarter. The pleasure he took in our pleasure gave me insight into what sheer joy being a father could be.

What do we do, then, to provide our children with substitutes for relatives? One way, I think, is to involve them in our own relationships, make them familiar with our friends, and bring them into contact with those friends. Children should benefit from knowing as many different adults as possible.

One of my friends who is a favorite of my sons is George Plimpton. His exploits as an amateur, playing football with the Lions, going a few rounds in the boxing ring, or doing a trapeze act in the circus, are the stuff children's dreams are made of, and every Fourth of July he has a picnic at the beach where he stages a fantastic display of fireworks. So George is a bit of a hero, and a few years back I was reading to Anderson about the French and Indian wars, in which one of the young fighters was a tall young American who would later become the first President of the United States. I figured Anderson would know who that was, and I waited for him to supply the name. He puzzled over it for a moment and then asked for a hint. "His name was General . . ." Still, the name was not forthcoming, so I gave a further hint. "General George . . ." Anderson's face lit up in victory. "Plimpton!" he cried.

If a friend is coming by for lunch with me, I tell my sons about that person, what he (or she) does for a living, what his interests are, how I came to know him, what I like about him, or even what

I don't like about him. Then after Carter and Anderson have met him, they are encouraged to express opinions or impressions later, and their judgments are discussed and respected. Children are great judges of character. I want them to know that adults can be wrong or foolish, and that they are free to make judgments of adults and to express them.

They ask questions about our friends. They are interested to know whether or not they have children, and they can tell whether or not those friends are interested in them. "Does he like children?" they often ask before someone arrives.

If they are to meet famous people, we talk about what they have done to create the fame. When we gave a party for Charlie Chaplin on his visit to America a few years ago, we talked about the fact that Mommy and Mrs. Chaplin had been friends since they were young girls, and that Mr. Chaplin would not look as he did in the films they already knew. They knew that Lillian Gish was coming, and we looked at pictures in our books on the history of movies so that when they met her, they could see in her lovely face the same tender beauty that they had seen in the pictures. Later we would take the boys to Town Hall to hear Miss Gish lecture about D. W. Griffith and her experiences in making films; she showed scenes from those films, and afterward they went backstage and talked with her about battle scenes in which Mr. Griffith made a hundred soldiers look like three hundred soldiers, or scenes in which a freezing Miss Gish floated on the Connecticut River on real ice floes.

They are not excluded. They feel that they are participating because they *are* participating. Even when they were tiny, if we entertained, they would remain downstairs, mingling with the guests until time for us to sit down for dinner. They held their own as conversationalists and their exits were made with some reluctance, a reluctance to part that was shared, I might say, by the guests themselves. On the evening of the party for the Chaplins, they stood beside us on the steps of our house, shaking hands to welcome the arriving guests, and somebody said to me that they had never seen children so well trained. Actually, they are not trained at all in that sense. We never suggested that they stand with us shaking hands. It was simply that when they saw us do it, it seemed natural to them to join us, for it was their house, too, and the guests were coming there to see them as well as us.

When the Lunts came to dinner, we followed the same process. Alfred Lunt and Lynn Fontanne are like gods to me, and I wanted the boys to know and understand why I had such awe and enthusiasm for them. They looked at photographs of the pair in many different roles from their long careers spanning more than fifty years, and they, too, looked forward to meeting these fabled creatures. When Miss Lynn spoke to my wife on the phone on the day after dinner, she said, speaking in her slow, precise way, "Alfred tells me that he had a most interesting conversation with your young man, who I believe he said was seven. They talked about Tolstoy, and Alfred thinks the child might be some kind of genius. Now, you know geniuses have a reputation for being somewhat difficult. Has he shown any signs of being difficult?"

He has not shown signs of being difficult, and he is not a genius. What he is, quite simply, is included.

They are involved in what we do. They are interested in my wife's paintings. They have their favorites among them; they make comments and suggestions, and when she has an exhibit, they want to be there. Several years ago, she had her first major museum retrospective at the Reading (Pennsylvania) Museum, and all of us drove down for it. It was very impressive indeed, and the boys were as overwhelmed as we were by the size and scope of the show. They walked around and listened to the comments of the people; they were very proud of their mother's accomplishment and they felt that they were a part of it.

They follow the progress of my work; they ask questions and they have opinions, and, if I complain that some editor wants to improve upon it, they share my indignation. "Why didn't she write it herself, then, if she's so smart?" Carter once asked.

What are we to do about making our children feel that they are members of the community they live in? It is not easy to feel a vital part of a city with millions of inhabitants. It is, in fact, a mountain of a problem, and it's not only a problem for our children; it's a problem for us. There was a time when most Americans lived in communities where they could not be unnoticed even if they wished to be. Their births were reported in the local paper; their growth and their illnesses were noted by interested neighbors; their weddings and other milestones were celebrated, and their deaths were mourned (or not, depending upon the effect they had had on the life around them). They may have been liked or disliked, but they were never ignored. In the supercities that so many of us now live in, we feel isolated, alone, and intimidated; we are dwarfed by the sheer size of the places, rendered faceless by the unseeing mass of its inhabitants, struck dumb from feeling that our outcries will go unheard. And, if we feel that no one is watching, our participation in the life of the community seems not to matter. One has a right not to be rendered invisible and can understand the impulse of the madwoman who stands on Broadway at nighttime shouting at the scurrying crowds, "Look at me. Look at me." One can understand how it comes about that armies of the young, doomed and futureless, go forth armed with spray cans to write their names in gigantic letters on subway cars, on public monuments, and on the side of mountains; one understands the lack of glory in their own identity that leads them in this celebration of themselves to invent new aliases with dash and flash in them, supplanting the common and promiseless names they answer to in ordinary life. In anonymity one ceases to be a citizen. And if we do not feel ourselves to be citizens, we cannot teach citizenship to our children. I believe that this lack of community has had a more devastating effect upon us than we realize. Man has always been a group creature; from the first we have known of him, he has run in a pack, living, hunting, fighting, celebrating, eating, and making decisions in company with others of his kind. We have that bonding instinct in us; it has been reinforced through centuries of use. Now our sense of isolation and estrangement comes in the midst of crowded populations. For a species that has never trusted the few hermits it has produced, it is strange that we have become hermits of the city, cut off from each other by a prevailing feeling of impotence.

Centuries of progress toward the realization of the significance of the individual have, by accident, brought us to a time of widespread loss of identity. Not to have a pack of one's own to run in or a group in which one is a member, known and counted upon, not to have a place and position on a familiar team, is a serious denial of an essential part of what one is made of.

And it hasn't happened just because there are so many of us. We have lately been hearing optimistic reports from Americans returning from visits to Red China, a nation far more populous than ours. Generally the visitors have expected to find a cruel and oppressive life in which multitudes were engaged in forced labor, performing like automatons or ants, sullen and dehumanized; and though such forced labor surely exists, and the "cultural revolutions" we hear about are certainly evidence that considerable dissension is there, still they have found a cheerful, enthusiastic, and forward-looking people, proud of their accomplishments, united in some sense of common purpose, and confident that they are building for the future. Obviously, their situation is not parallel to ours. They are escaping from a painful and oppressive past, and they know that conditions are better for them than they were for their parents. More importantly, there is nothing in their heritage, political or philosophical, that would encourage them to believe in either the rights of the individual or the expectation of personal fulfillment, as does Western cultural tradition. But that a feeling of shared enterprise exists and that this commitment has produced enormous progress very quickly seems to be true. What we require is to find a sense of fulfillment as individuals and a sense that we are useful to others and engaged in some common enterprises with them.

We began as a rural country and remained so until a few decades ago. Local matters were settled (for better or worse) locally, and local attitudes prevailed. In the beginning the citizens gathered at town hall meetings, argued things out, and then voted. It was easy enough to know that your vote counted. Today we still vote, at least every four years, though rarely on local issues, and, in New York, where I live, apart from the excitement when a controversial or glamorous figure like John Lindsay is running for mayor, we don't feel that life-and-death matters are at stake. Back home we used to take our country politics very seriously indeed. If it had been left to me, every year would have been election year. I had violently partisan feelings about the candidates for sheriff; I listened avidly to their speeches at the church picnics; I would happily applaud our family friend, Mr. Harvey Norris, when he promised to make the best county supervisor Beat One ever had, and I miss the participation that existed then.

I think we owe it to ourselves to form opinions, to participate in our own minds, even if we know for sure that our vote will never be recorded. To exist only as a nonperson in a Kafka-type world requires a certain amount of complicity on our part, after all. We can always refuse to go along—in the privacy of our mind, at least, even if it means refusing to accept reality. "I *am* in charge!" we can say, "the pilot of my soul, the captain of my destiny. I am free in *here!*" we can say, eyes gleaming as we tap our fingers against our old noggin. "I make up my own mind. And what I think is . . ." We may end up quite mad of course, and be shut up somewhere, but in the more important way we will be free.

At my house, the boys watch Walter Cronkite with us every night, and we talk about the rights and wrongs of what we see and hear. I don't think it has ever occurred to either of them that their opinions are not being taken into consideration, and I hope that they never begin to assume such a thing.

They take pride in our city. Carter is furious if old buildings of distinction are torn down, and they have been known to remind strangers that it is not right to drop litter in the park. Even in large cities we can, with our children, make a point of knowing as many people in our neighborhood as we can. They are also people with wives, husbands, homes, worries, names; and they don't like being strangers any more than we do. We can take some small interest in our neighbors. My kids have always been delighted that they can say "Hello" to Policeman Paul down the street, and they are proud that he knows their names. Soon after a new stationery store opened in our block, Anderson said of the owner, "Mr. Jensen is in his store all the time; he never gets to be home with his family," and I said, "Maybe he doesn't have a family." "Oh, yes, he does," Anderson said. "He has a wife and a boy and a girl. I saw them in there one day." Lack of involvement is not natural nor indifference the norm. He had kept his eyes open and he was interested. When he got his live snake for his sixth birthday (it's what he wanted), he let it curl around his fist and insisted that we set out to show it off around the neighborhood. We went to the barbershop, the stationery store, the coffee shop, the candy store, a men's shop, the florist, the bank—anywhere we were known—and we stopped to visit with every doorman who had a free moment. I'm afraid we even exhibited it to a few horrified strangers.

All children, I suppose, are interested in the history of a place, and that interest should be encouraged at the time it first appears. They go from "Where did I come from?" to "Where did the earth come from?" and "How did we come to be here?" Those questions are often not encouraged. It seems too complicated to answer, and sometimes by the time they get to geography in school it has become a dry exercise, something that no longer has any connection with themselves. My boys know (because they wanted to know) quite a lot about how New York came to be New York, and when we've visited other cities, we've read about those places and looked for the landmarks. When we went to Kansas City, they were afraid there would be a tornado because Dorothy in *The Wizard of Oz* came from Kansas and was blown away in such a storm. I assured them that tornadoes happened rarely, and they believed me until we got to the Crown Center Hotel and they (naturally) turned on the television set only to find in progress a report on the devastation wrought by a twister in a nearby hamlet. So now they know a bit about Midwestern climate conditions, and the knowledge is personal. While we were there we drove to Independence, Missouri, and took pictures of each other in front of former President Truman's house; then we went to the Truman Library and took pictures of Truman's grave. There was some confusion when we discovered that Anderson, then five, was under the impression that the grave he was photographing belonged to our family friend Truman Capote, but we got that straightened out for the benefit of history. When they get home, they paste their pictures in a book as a record of their travels, and they do it not because anybody urges them to but because they want to, and because it means something to them.

We are avid sightseers, and we want to know what we are seeing. We don't just wander through and look at picturesque places—what I heard an American woman in Rome once refer to as "all this darling quaintness"—we want to know what they mean, what kind of people brought them into being, and what happened in them. In New Orleans we read about New Orleans. We learn that the Spanish built the Cabildo, where the French later signed the papers of the Louisiana Purchase, and that it was the Spanish who built their houses around patios with fountains and flowers in them. Jackson fought the British nearby, and slaves were auctioned off on the very corner across from our hotel. In Natchez, Mississippi, we read Natchez history, we go through as many splendid houses as we can cram into our days, and we see the home of General John A. Quitman, for whom my home town had been named. We are eager to see Longwood, also known as Nutt's Folly in honor of Dr. Nutt who started its construction. We already know of the house from architecture books; it is an incredible octagonal fantasy of a house, left unfinished because of the intervention of the Civil War. We spend a morning there, and Carter and Mommy decide that it is their favorite house of abode in all the world. In Puerto Rico we get a book on Puerto Rican history; we explore the huge and ancient fort; we run our fingers along the iron of the cannons and try to imagine them firing upon pirate ships. We walk along streets that have been there for centuries and that have known the tread of millions of vanished men of other races, colors, and tongues, and we feel a kinship with the panorama of human history. The boys go over the pictures in their scrapbooks, relive the high points of their travel, and feel rooted in the world.

For persons with active and inquiring minds, there's not much time for feeling alienated. Children start out with minds like that, and it's up to us not to let that go.

We are beginning, I think, to respect our regional differences, to enjoy the great variety of landscape in our land, the different traditions among our people. We've discovered the beauty of folk art and folk music, and we've begun to be aware of preserving something of our colorful heritage.

When I was in high school in New Orleans, we observed

something called Brotherhood Week, and as a part of the observance, we were addressed by a priest, a rabbi, and a Protestant clergyman. The rabbi impressed me considerably. He spoke of Keats's line, "A thing of beauty is a joy forever," and he went on to ask, "What is beauty?" He offered as an answer "diversity within unity." Works of art are, of course, composed of contrasting colors, forms, forces, or ideas, each valid in its own right, brought together to form a harmonious whole. Just so, he said, people of diverse backgrounds, races, habits, and inheritances can, without surrendering their own particular customs or colorations, exist in harmony. His speech struck me (and stuck with me) because it contained a new idea for me. I had thought, as most people thought, that the aim of our American civilization was to perfect the melting pot. That is, we Americans were to be the models of the world; those of other nations who brought to our shores their talents, their pasts, their futures, would as soon as possible lose all former coloration and become a recognizable and established and well-defined new thing—an American. I suppose I pictured them seeking, in all haste, to become rather like me. I had, until that moment, prided myself on my tolerance. Until those others had had their chance to become like me (I exaggerate my personal ego in this, my own ethnocentrism, but it is in order to make a point) it behooved me to be tolerant of them while they made their effort. The rabbi gave me a jolt. His concept carried no obligation that they become like me. They already had something that was worth holding onto, in itself valuable and beautiful, and, if that was true, tolerance was not what was called for. Tolerance implied a certain condescension. One tolerates from an exalted or superior position; it therefore followed that if Italians, or Spaniards, or the Irish, Jews, or blacks already had something to be proud of, if they needed to feel no obligation to shed their identities, then toleration was inappropriate. What was in order was not toleration but respect.

It reminded me of something I'd learned years before when I heard Mr. Ezra Tucker say, "The Good Lord in His wisdom fixed it so that each person has different taste. Otherwise, every man would have wanted my Trudy." It came as a revelation to me that there existed someone, even so unprepossessing a person as Mr. Ezra Tucker, actually capable of wanting his Trudy.

Since then, people have begun to take pride in ethnic origins. No longer need children of foreign-born parents be ashamed that another language is spoken at home. We have become aware that all peoples have had great histories; every country has its own splendid pageant of the past; we have realized that native dances, folklore, and folkways have sprung from something colorful and expressive in the lives of those people and are to be prized and preserved as national treasures. Blacks have discovered for themselves that black is beautiful, and when they discovered it, *we* discovered it. We have, I hope, found that our differences are as precious as our resemblances and that those differences need not divide us, that they can, in fact, delight us, educate us, and expand our own visions.

Those differences disappear all too rapidly, in any case. In most families, unless there are marked physical racial characteristics few remaining clues to those national origins can be found after a couple of generations. We should enjoy our distinctions while we can. My children sometimes come home from school and announce happily that a new boy from India or Africa or Japan has joined the class. In New York we have vast populations of every nationality, and most of them have some day set aside during which they march up Fifth Avenue. The parade ties up the city traffic for that day and we complain bitterly, but if such days were banished, our lives would be the poorer for it.

Not long ago when Adam Green, the son of our friends Phyllis Newman and Adolph Green, was to be bar mitzvahed, my family and I were invited, and we went without much prior knowledge of bar mitzvahs. I knew that there was a party with an abundance of food and that at some point the boy would say, "Today I am a man," but I had no idea of what a moving occasion it could be, or that it was one of singular significance for our peculiar times. In the ceremony the boy stands with his father and mother and the elders of the temple and partakes of the history, tradition, law, and faith of an ancient people. It is an acknowledgment on his part that he owes something to his heritage and that he will continue to serve that heritage in his time and through his descendants. At the point of coming into man's estate he is being reminded that he is to take his place in the councils of those elders; he is to bring his judgment and his maturity to the service of the community.

And that, surely, is what we've been talking about. We need, all of us, to devise, somehow, some sort of emotional or psychological or spiritual bar mitzvah for ourselves and for our children, in which we vow to take our place in the continuing history of man, to raise our voices in the councils of our lawmakers, to be concerned citizens and decent neighbors in our communities, to seek after truth and good will and common sense, to serve right and justice and fair-mindedness, to maintain some happy balance between humility and pride, to cry as often as we must, to laugh whenever we can, and to have a hot meal at least once a day.

9

Some Dangers of Family Life

*Lizzie Borden took an ax
And gave her mother forty whacks;
When she saw what she had done
She gave her father forty-one!*
                    —*Children's song*

When we speak of the contrast between our days and earlier times, we sometimes sound as if we are mourning the passing of some mythological golden age. Perhaps there have been golden ages—I don't know—certainly there have been periods of general prosperity, or of optimism, or of expansion, or of relative contentment, but I suspect that ages are golden only in retrospect, and then only from a special point of view. Looking back from the perspective of troubled days, we are likely to paint a rosy picture of earlier eras, when a different set of perplexities prevailed.

I write with some feeling of nostalgia about my youth and my large family, but I am under no illusion that I grew up in any golden age. Nor did my father. The Victorian era has been held up to us as a high point in the history of the family. Large families were usual, and we picture them bustling, busy, devoted, and contented, grouped around a cheery fireside in comfortable drawing rooms. The institution of the family was then more secure, more stable, and more influential, but it also labored under a heavy burden of hypocrisy and pretension. Conformity and outward respectability were highly valued, but behind those sober façades wild passions smoldered and inner feelings were suppressed and denied. Many lived secret lives, others burst out into bizarre behavior, and some drowned in the attempt to stay on the surface. Those family members who had unconventional leanings, those who did not fit in, were often, in a sort of silent conspiracy, simply sacrificed on the altar of respectability. The daughter who wanted to be a doctor, or who refused to marry, or who sought some other role for which there was not a currently acceptable mold would be allowed to waste away in an upstairs room, taking refuge in a series of psychosomatic illnesses, while other family members assured everyone that she suffered from a delicate constitution. *That* was a perfectly respectable role. The unconventional son—the dreamer, the questioner, the iconoclast—could be driven to drink while Mother murmured softly about bearing her cross with Christian fortitude. The black sheep was such a recognized and accepted role that any offspring or sibling at all "different" could be cast into it with equanimity by his family, without their losing any of their status in the community.

Tolstoy said, "All happy families resemble one another. Every unhappy family is unhappy each in its own fashion." The happy families I've known have supported each other, learned from each other, and cherished one another's good opinions. They have had their own standards, their own ways of talking and thinking, their own jokes; and when the world seemed to differ from them, they confronted it with the cheerful confidence that they were right and the world was wrong. When a family is unhappy, they can behave toward each other in cruel and cutting ways that they would never exercise toward an outsider. Out of pain and frustration, or fear, family members can gang up on one member and make him the scapegoat for all their negative feelings. They can even drive each other mad. Insanity can, it seems, really be quite contagious. If a father or mother has a particularly distorted view of reality, they can overtly or unconsciously instill that point of view in their child, or so disorient him that he forms his own distortion.

In our community there was a family named Armstead, which was, by any judgment, totally uncivilized. We figured they were all born crazy, though just which ones were really over the line and which ones were only infected with the others' wild irrationality, we could not know. The head of the clan, the tallest and the toughest, was the mother, Kassie. Kassie Armstead had been a Tuck, and the Tucks had been mad for as long as anybody could remember. "Bad blood in that family goes way back," we used to say. Kassie's craziness, though, was of museum quality even by Tuck standards. She was a classroom example of just how far a Tuck could go without being locked up. There were times when the school bus would stop at their place to drop the Armstead children, and the rest of us would gaze wonderingly at the spectacle of an Armstead family fight. Mrs. Armstead would be on the warpath and Mr. Armstead, in a losing battle, would be fighting back. Sometimes some of her brothers would have dropped over to help out, armed with sticks, stones, and other throwable objects. As the Armstead children piled off the bus, they would instantly choose sides and enter the fray, some for the father, some for the mother. Except for Rufus. He stood alone, pained, ashamed, and somehow above it. Rufus had the makings of a decent fellow, and, given a fair chance elsewhere and later on, he would become one. He would walk through the flying debris and into the house without acknowledging the profane shouts and insults that filled the air like an exchange of arrows. Whether he was born of sturdier stuff, a throwback to a better man somewhere in their sorry history, or whether the horror of living within a constant tornado simply built in him a resolve to become a rational, useful citizen, I do not know.

Regina Armstead, whom we have already met as Helen of Troy, was her mother's chosen favorite. The other daughters could ruin their skin by going out in the sun, but Regina was not to risk her beauty. The others could content themselves with the ginghams and cheap cottons that were standard wear, but Regina must have ruffles and flowered silks and taffetas. To acquire such a wardrobe in those poverty-stricken times required some talent for larceny, and, crazy or not, Kassie was equal to the task. She would order a dress from the Sears Roebuck catalogue. When it arrived, she would write indignantly to the mail-order company complaining of nondelivery; she would state that in the meantime she had changed her mind and would like some other dress instead. By continuing in this way for some time, she managed to build up a considerable collection of finery. Once Regina came to an all-day sing at the church in a clinging pink satin evening gown with rhinestone trim; she was the belle of the day, surrounded at all times by a swarm of goggle-eyed swains, and, though my sisters sneered at the unsuitability of it, I thought it was gorgeous and urged those scornful sisters to copy her style.

Kassie, not surprisingly, held in contempt other people's attempts to conduct their lives with decorum, and whenever any of our neighbors suffered any fall from grace (such as a sudden marriage when premature pregnancy was a possibility; a case of adultery discovered; or an arrest for the sale of bootleg whiskey), she took it as her special responsibility to see that the wrongdoing did not pass without comment. If she suddenly showed up at church, singing what was called "alto"—which really meant a kind of loud piercing counterpoint harmony—we knew she was there because she had a scandal to announce. Or if she couldn't wait for Sunday, she would dab two red circles of rouge on her cheeks and set out to spread the news, her eyes bright with venomous glee. The noise of her approach would reach us when she was still quite far off, for she had a grown son by a former marriage who was not right in the head (being right in the head was a relative matter among Tucks and Armsteads, but Maynard was violently off) and he would run ahead of her along the road, as excited as a bird dog, and she would call out to him, "Maynard, you Maynard, you come back here!" Maynard paid no attention (he never paid attention unless she hit him with the six-foot stick she carried for that purpose), and we would scurry into the house and bolt the door at the sight of him, but he would run up onto the porch, bounce up and down so that the house rattled, stick his face in the window and utter a prolonged maniacal laugh which seemed like an evil caricature of Kassie's own. Kassie would come puffing after him, beat him back with her stick before the door was opened, all the time yelling to reassure us, "He ain't gonna hurt you! Down Maynard, down, I say." Maynard would snarl and swear and go around in circles, hitting out at the stick, but finally he would settle down on the porch, grumbling to himself, muttering threats and curses, and Kassie would sweep in with her news.

Anthropologist Jules Henry in *Pathways to Madness* documents the proposition that it is quite possible for a person to go crazy not simply as an individual and not only from the inside out (that is, as the result of unresolved internal conflict), but as a part of a group—in the cases he studies, the group is the family—whose other members subtly coerce him into a role and then stigmatize him for that role.

The child so cast may not recognize it, even as he accepts it. It is done, after all, in the name of love. The child who is told that he is bad will believe it and will go out of his way to prove it. When he is mistreated by parents, he assumes that it is his fault, not that of the parents. Children, after all, think everything is their fault, parents' maltreatment, parents' bad behavior, parents' alcoholism, even the sickness or death of parents.

While we're talking about the perils of family life, I might as well mention the melancholy fact that most murders occur within families. One is far more likely to be done in by one's mate, or even by one's child, than by any bushy-haired stranger bent on mayhem. This really isn't a new situation; after all, who else cares enough? One of the sons of the First Family of the Universe killed the other son, and on a casual tour through the Greek classics you run into enough family slaughter to suggest that we've descended not from the friendly ape but from the black widow spider. Freud, of course, found in that body of literature more than enough outrages to give names to all the complexes he discovered for us.

Today, of course, we read about such things all the time. It happens among the rich and among the poor, to the respectable as well as to the disorderly. A New Jersey father, hard-working accountant and Sunday school teacher, pressured by illness or financial disaster, slashes the throats of his wife, children, mother-in-law, and family dog, then disappears. A Long Island mother smothers her children and cuts her wrists. A father argues with his son about the taking of drugs and ends up shooting the boy he wanted to save. A young man, well mannered and polite, kills his parents, sets fire to the house, and sits calmly waiting for the police to arrive.

I have known of family fights and family feuds and family beatings, but the first family murder that touched my life was an especially sensational one, famous for a time throughout the state. A few years ago I was visiting Eudora Welty in Jackson, and she mentioned a woman she knew of who had gone mad and had been sent to Whitfield, Mississippi's mental institution. According to the story Eudora had heard, the woman was one day playing bridge with other inmates including a couple of murderesses, and she suddenly put down her cards and said to one of her companions, "I refuse to play one more card, Ouida Keeton, until you tell me what you did with the rest of your mother!" (Parts of the senior Mrs. Keeton's body were never found.) I asked Eudora, "Would you like to know what Ouida did with the rest of her mother?" and Eudora said, "I certainly would. We speculated about it for years." I said, "I can tell you, because Ouida was a relative of mine." Eudora, who is, besides being a distinguished writer, a gentlewoman with exquisite manners, was covered with embarrassment, and protested that she'd never have dreamed of mentioning it if she'd known. I was able to reassure her that there was no cause for dismay. I'd always taken some morbid delight in the case, for it had made me at ten or eleven a celebrity around the schoolyard.

I stretched the truth slightly in claiming Ouida (named for the English novelist) as a blood relation. Actually, we were connected only through marriage. My mother's sister was married to Ouida's brother. The Keetons were people of substantial means, and there, I believe, the trouble began. Ouida, who was, in my judgment, extremely pretty, charming, and friendly, got into a dispute with her mother over a large sum of money and the whole matter was about to become public knowledge. Mrs. Keeton, in any case, had never been easy to get along with, so Ouida (with the assistance of another person who was never named) shot her mother one night, sawed her up into sections, and disposed of the body —Mrs. Keeton was not a small woman—in several imaginative ways. A couple of thighs, unfortunately for the delightful Ouida, were abandoned in the woods, where they were stumbled upon by a man out squirrel hunting. It was Ouida's imagination that did her in; at one point she told investigators that an elderly woman in a long black veil, carrying a gun, had kidnaped her mother. The police officers, trying to be gentlemen about it, looked for but did not find any trace of a veiled villainess; they had, finally and reluctantly, to face facts, and Ouida, well born and enchanting though she might have been, was taken into custody. It was all very shocking and hard to believe and it stayed in the newspapers for a long time. She was often compared most favorably with the less attractive Yankee lady, Miss Lizzie Borden, whose crime in some ways paralleled hers. When she was out on bail before the trial, she came with my aunts and cousins to my grandmother's house, and I happened to be there. I was fascinated but, I confess, terrified, and when Ouida, at one point, said to my cousin Doris Flowers, "I have an idea," and they whispered together for a moment, I suspected that I was the subject of the conversation. When they went to the kitchen and came back with a knife and a container of salt, I was convinced of it, and only my extreme sense of decorum prevented my taking off across the cotton field. The idea was, it developed, altogether innocent; my grandmother had a tree loaded down with little green apples; the knife was for peeling and the salt for salting.

My schoolmates were full of questions, naturally enough, and the teachers themselves were not above mentioning the scandal, knowing that I would tell everything I had heard at home (and then some). The trial was sensational, and it was decided that the best thing to do—Southerners don't like to execute ladies if they can possibly avoid it, especially not ladies of Ouida's class—was just to declare her insane and send her to Whitfield, where she has remained for the last thirty-six years, making herself useful in the library, the last time I heard, and, of course, improving her hand at bridge.

Now that I've offended my relatives by telling that story when they've been trying to live it down ("Buddy, I hope you're not going to drag up all that Ouida Keeton stuff," my sister Grace said, when I was telling her about this book), I might as well go on and tell about two others. A year or so before I married I was visiting down home, and just as I arrived at my sister Annie Laura's house in Quitman the local newspaper came, and in it was a very brief item, which, with necessary alterations, went something like this: "CLARKE COUNTY RESIDENT SLAIN. According to Sheriff Preston Cooper [my cousin, not the Preston Cooper who is my brother] Billy Ray Leeks, 24, was slain in an incident in Clarke County yesterday. He is survived by his widow, Mrs.

Celeste Leeks, 23, and their two children, Billy, Jr., 3, and Bonnie Sue, 2. Funeral services will be held Monday morning at 10 o'clock at the Mount Hope Methodist Church." Of course, this Billy Ray was a cousin of mine, a couple of times removed— almost everybody in Clarke County is a cousin, if you look closely enough—and therefore also a cousin of the sheriff, and so was, for that matter, the widow, on her side. No mention was made in this newspaper account of the fact that the widow shot him. In such "incidents" there is almost always a struggle over a gun (usually some drinking has been involved), the gun goes off, and everybody feels "just terrible" about it. It is, in places where all the participants are known to everybody else, the practice to deal quite sensibly with it: there's no use doing anything silly like locking poor Celeste up—she's upset enough as it is—and making total orphans of those two children, so everybody just says what an awful, unfortunate incident it was and that Billy Ray sure will be missed and soon it's referred to as that "trouble they had out at the Leekses."

Naturally I had told my bride-to-be about both these cases, among others that I haven't space for here, and I rather suspect that she thought of them as amusing stories, not to be taken literally. Nobody ever believes you if you tell the truth, and besides most people suspect, often quite rightly, that writers are congenital liars.

When she went down to meet my relatives, we were at the same sister's house and I asked Tom, my brother-in-law, who was the town marshal, "Have you had any murders lately?" "No," he said, "we haven't." Then he said, "I guess you heard about the trouble Ed Hollenbeck had." Ed Hollenbeck was a cousin of the dead Leeks boy, and—do I have to tell you?—a cousin of mine. "Well," Tom said, "according to Ed, him and his wife were laying across the bed and she was mashing blackheads out of his back—" (You know that has to be true; nobody would think of making up a line like that) "And she got up, went into the other room, came back with the gun, and said she was going to kill herself. Ed, he tried to take the gun away from her and it went off. Killed her. And Ed had two bullets in his head." I noticed Gloria was paying close attention. "What did you do with Ed?" I asked. "Well," Tom answered, "we had to take him over to Whitfield to get the bullets taken out. Oh, by the way, on the way over there he asked me how you were doing, and I told him you were coming down, and he said be sure to tell you 'Hi.'" I looked over at my future wife, and her eyes were as wide open as they would ever be. She saw, at last, that it was all true, every single word of it.

Because the family reflects the tensions of its times, the Victorian child was likely to suffer from the hypocrisy and the repressive spirit then prevailing. Because ours is an alienated and depersonalized society many of today's parents lack warmth or any real respect for the child. Many of them fear that they don't know how to parent, and they therefore fear the child. This is a fairly new phenomenon; in earlier days parents, for better or worse, did not doubt that they knew how it should be done. They simply copied the practice of their parents, and rarely worried about it. If the children turned out badly, they didn't think of it as their fault as we do. We are both more enlightened and less enlightened than that. So much study has been made that we're quite confused, and look to the specialists to advise us, and, sometimes, the more books we read, the more our apprehension grows.

Right or wrong, our parents were at least positive. Few today dare to be positive about anything; this insecurity is sensed by the children, and their own apprehension grows accordingly. Lack of respect for the child, the absence of delight in him, is communicated either by harshness or by a hypocritical overcoddling and overprotectiveness which serves to cripple his normal urge for independence. I have known selfish or guilt-ridden parents who expressed to their child great fears for his safety every time he left the house. Trains collide. Planes fall. Lightning strikes. Every sneeze suggests a fatal disease. Such treatment encourages timidity and feelings of dependence, dependence upon the very parents who are least dependable.

We have been living in affluent times in America, and we have showered our children with luxuries. Now, if we treat ourselves in the same way, if we provide ourselves with an overabundance of cars, clothes, record players, and the like, it would be peculiar if we denied them to our children, but each parent ought to carefully examine his behavior and his motives in this regard. All too often children are given expensive things out of some sense of inadequacy on the part of the parent, out of fear, or feelings of guilt, or as a substitute for the time, the attention, or the love that is due them. If this is true, the child will sense it and will, in fact, resent both the gifts and the giver.

Whether or not our children learn to value and enjoy their possessions depends largely upon how we ourselves value and enjoy the things we have. It depends upon how much we coddle or overindulge ourselves. Often the best thing we could do for our children is to determine whether we are constantly giving ourselves things we neither need nor enjoy, and trying in that way to fill some need for love or some lack of emotional security. Sometimes a father will say, "When I was a kid, I had no bike, and my son's going to have the best bike in the block," which is, as far as it goes, fair enough. He should be sure, though, that the child wants a bike, is ready for a bike, and that the bike he buys isn't more than is called for. If these conditions are not there, then he may simply ruin his child's normal chance of enjoying the bike. To overwhelm a child with gifts, to anticipate his desires, robs him of a chance to have desires, to enjoy those desires, and to have anticipations of his own. Whether or not it spoils the child, I don't know; I do know it spoils his pleasure in things. Half the fun of getting a bike is the poring over catalogues, the shopping around, the thinking about it, the deciding, the changing of the mind, and, in the end, participating in the final selection and purchase.

We must be honest with our children. If we are false, if we lie, they know it; and if we lie and they don't know it, it's worse, because they have to distrust their own perceptions in order to believe us. If what they see for themselves, what their minds tell them, is different from what we tell them, then it takes a certain amount of distortion to accept as truth that which they experience as false. If they sense that the face the parents turn toward them is not real, if they know that parents do not behave as they *say* one should behave, then they become skeptical and cynical about all authority, all moral instruction, indeed all human motives. It does not hurt grown people now and then to admit that they have been mistaken. Our child will not respect us less for knowing that we are sometimes confused or impulsive or angry or that there are things that we don't know. He will respect us much more for our honesty in admitting it; more importantly, it will help him to accept his own right to be confused or angry or not to know.

I can't spell, for instance. I never could, and it has sometimes been my undoing. In Quitman, if you wanted your wedding to be reported in the *Clarke County Tribune,* you had to write it up yourself and send it in. When my sister Marie married Roger Graham, I knew that she wouldn't bother, so I did it, figuring that she would not know who the reporter was. When it came out, though, there was no mystery about it. The editor had corrected all my wrongly spelled words except the proper names, and nobody else would have thought that the groom's name was spelled Rojur Grayum. My sons, both of whom already spell quite well, take some friendly pleasure in my disability. It's a part of knowing that we can't all be perfect, that all of us do some things better than other things, and when I'm helping them with homework, they will sometimes tease me by asking, with an earnestly straight face, how many "c"s there are in "across," or whether the "i" comes before the "e" after "c."

In the same way, they cheerfully forgive me for being a terrible baseball player. Until we started going to the park to play with their pal Michael Wolfson and his father, I'd only had one experience with the game. That occurred in high school when I cut across the baseball field on my way to a play rehearsal and somehow managed to get my jaw knocked out of its socket by a stray ball. Michael's father is an expert, a marvel of grace and coordination, while I seem always to have worn the wrong glasses. It doesn't matter. It's the spirit that counts, and we have fun.

When I was in school, all the boys seemed to be obsessed with sex. Any time that adults were not present, sexual remarks, speculations, boasting, and the crudest sort of fantasies were tossed about like spitballs. What was remarkable about it was that the coarseness of it was in reverse ratio to the official views of sex we were given. Farm children discover the mechanics of sex very early; they have the example of the barnyard before them, and the insistent brutality of the way it was talked about by the boys came about, I think, because of the prudery and hypocrisy with which it was handled by adults. It seemed to them a dirty thing to be boasted about with leers and sneers, precisely because it had been covered up so determinedly by adults. Most boys had been told by their fathers that if they masturbated they would go mad. I suppose that some of those fathers actually believed that; after all, fifty or sixty years ago, there were doctors who believed it, but I know that few of the boys believed it. It only made them feel guilty and sordid about a perfectly natural pleasure, and I suspect that most of them knew that the fathers who told them such things did so out of some feeling of shame of their own, and would have been dismayed to learn that their sons actually did not masturbate—would, indeed, quite rightly have worried about whether something was wrong with the boys. Most fathers, too, on discovering their son experimenting in the garage with the neighbor's daughter, would have felt called upon to punish the son and give him a firm talking-to about the wickedness of it, but would then have boasted around the neighborhood about the boy's precociousness.

I am not, God knows, recommending that fathers do what my father did, and keep their sons filled in on their own sexual adventures. There's a point somewhere along there where honesty falls off into exhibitionism. It's just that I don't think children should be taught one set of values when you really expect them to live by some other set, and since sexual curiosity begins quite naturally very early on, blessed is the son who has a father who is neither embarrassed nor ashamed to answer the questions calmly and easily as they arise, and blessed is the son who feels free to ask.

One day it was reported to me that Carter had used a "dirty" word, and I should speak to him about it. I asked Carter if he knew what it meant; he burst into tears and said that he did not. He had learned it at school and had introduced it into a social conversation. First of all, I assured him that he had done nothing wrong, nothing to be ashamed of or embarrassed about, and that I did not believe that words were "dirty." Attitudes might be dirty (in the brutal sense) or intentions might be dirty, but words were only tools used to describe something. How could they in themselves be dirty? I told him that the word he used was slang for making love; that making love was neither dirty, shameful, nor anything to be afraid of or even mystified about. Further, that I might, in speaking lightly to a friend, use that word instead of saying "make love." One must not be frightened of words. What matters is how they are used and the attitudes they convey. I went on to say that none of this was intended to suggest that he should continue to use the word. It would embarrass adults and it would be inappropriate in a child's vocabulary. Those children who say it in school do so because such words seem to them to have some mystery and magic in them. The child feels that it makes him seem bigger, older, more knowing. It's a cover-up for ignorance, a kind of showing-off, or pretending an ease and sophistication he can't possibly feel, and he uses the word because the word and the act it represents are forbidden, not because he actually feels comfortable about either the word or the meaning of it.

If all this sounds too complicated to be explained to a child, then I assure you that it is not. The point is that it should be explained at the time he seeks an explanation, for he has at that time been thinking about it, and is ready for some guidance. I wouldn't call the child in from play and embark on a lecture, nor would I volunteer much more information than he seemed to be looking for at that moment, but there is nothing in the above that a six-year-old in that situation cannot grasp.

Children look to us to show them what the limits are. They count on us for guidance and for some curbing of their destructive impulses. When Anderson was a tiny tot, I came upon him in a temper tantrum kicking his nurse. I was shocked and I told him so. I told him that other people spank their children, and though I didn't believe in spanking or think it was necessary, this business of attacking the nurse was too serious a matter to let pass, and that I would, if I ever knew of his doing it again, resort to spanking. He listened, as he always did, and he understood.

A few days later I walked in on a repeat of the earlier scene. There he was, in a rage, kicking away. We looked at each other, both trapped. Both knew something had to be done. I took him into another room and repeated my feelings about spanking (which is, when you come down to it, nothing more than a big person striking a smaller one), I even quoted George Bernard Shaw ("If you strike a child . . . strike it in anger. . . . A blow in cold blood neither can nor should be forgiven"), explaining that

I felt terrible about what I was doing, but I told him (in what the nurse said was a tearful voice) that I felt I had to do it. He nodded solemnly, and, with a hesitant and unwilling hand, I actually spanked my child, feeling miserable and a failure and vowing that I would never let it happen again. At first I thought the strong little fellow wasn't going to cry, and I don't think I could have borne it if he had lain across my lap taking that spanking without tears. He did cry, of course, and I didn't spank hard, and when it was over, I repeated the whole discussion all over again.

A little later, to make sure that he understood that no ill feelings were involved, I took him on an outing to the park. As we went out the door, his little paw in mine, he looked up at me, grinning with pride, and said in a spirit of shared camaraderie, " 'Member when you 'panked me?"

10

———◆⟨∞⟩◆———

Coming of Age

"The foundation of morality is to have done, once and for all, with lying." —T. H. HUXLEY

"Alas, I have done nothing this day: What? Have you not lived? It is not only the fundamental but the noblest of your occupations." —MONTAIGNE

Children seek moral guidance, and many parents in today's world are themselves too confused about their own beliefs to know how to give it. When children raise ethical questions, they are told, "You'll understand it someday." They won't understand it someday. What they'll do is stop asking, even of themselves. Once, Carter selected a children's book on history for his bedtime reading, and we read about Peter the Great and the failure of his attempts to westernize Russia. He had tried to accomplish this from the top down, without doing anything about land reform or about the huge class of serfs, not realizing that the progress of the rest of Europe had to do with the rise of a middle class and a bettering of the conditions of workingmen. I looked at Carter, wondering if this was too much to follow. He wanted to hear more.

The book mentioned Tolstoy. Tolstoy, as I've already said, was someone Carter knew about, not only because of *War and Peace* but because he knew that I had had occasion to correspond with

Tolstoy's daughter, now in her nineties, who is the founder of a Russian refugee colony at Nyack, New York. Tolstoy, it said, had tried to free his serfs and to turn his estates and his income over to them, and he had not been able to, not only because the serfs mistrusted his motives but because his wife would not agree. "That wasn't very nice of her," Carter said, so I tried to explain Countess Tolstoy's side of the matter. She had thirteen children, and she wanted them to have the same kind of schooling and opportunities as others of their class. It would, doubtless, have been noble and saintly of her to have agreed with her husband to give everything up, but sainthood is a lot to expect of mere mortals, particularly a mere mortal mother with thirteen children to think of.

Carter himself drew a parallel that had obviously been in his mind: "Like it's not really right that we have this big house, when Arthur lives in that one room with his mother and brother, but if we give it up, then we won't have it." Arthur was a friend who lived in East Harlem; Carter had been to his apartment and, clearly, had been disturbed by its poverty. We talked about the complexities of right and wrong and about the responsibilities of those who *have* to do what they can for those who do not have. Then he crawled across my lap, wrapped his arm across my chest, and said with emotion in his voice, "You make me very happy." He had already given thought, though not verbal expression, to the question of justice and Arthur's poverty and his own relative comfort, and he was grateful to have it recognized and acknowledged that such questions are normal and desirable and not dilemmas to be thrust away in shame, into the unconscious.

Sometimes the only answer to a question is there is no answer, but that is already the beginning of an answer.

Once great men made speeches crediting all their accomplishments to the principles taught at their mother's knees, and to their father's hard labor, which had enabled them to get through school. Those speeches, which used to produce tears and provide inspiration, would now, I suppose, be as funny to a modern audience as the passion of Portnoy's mother. And yet they were true. People, at least poor people, did work hard to earn their child a chance at a place in the sun. They dreamed of giving him a life "better" than their own, little knowing that this goal gave their own lives a meaning and a purpose that their "luckier" children would never know. They did teach principles because they lived in a time when it was possible to believe in them.

Today, though, we consider ourselves too knowledgeable, too "sophisticated," it seems, to talk of naïve matters like right and wrong, and if that is so, then we've educated ourselves into abysmal ignorance. It is true that right and wrong are often relative concepts. What may be wrong for me may be fine for you. A sober-faced Mr. Arthur Griffin came up to my sister after church one Sunday and spoke to her gravely. "Miss Grace, I just have to ask you something. Somebody told me he saw you up at Lake Clarko going in mixed bathing, and I told him it couldn't be so." "Mixed bathing" meant that men and women, all modestly clothed, of course, in bathing suits of the thirties, had been swimming in the same lake. Poor Grace had to admit that it was true. She had seen nothing wrong with it, but Mr. Griffin turned away without a word, deeply grieved and disillusioned in the face of rampant immorality. This is, admittedly, a trivial example, and I do not advocate that we return to simplistic standards or forget everything we have learned; but I can't help believing that some principles do remain that can be passed on to our children. I believe that the young need to be instructed somehow in the lessons we have learned from the past.

It is our responsibility, not the school's. Also, school is basically a group activity, and the child needs to have another world in which he is known and recognized as an individual, in which he can learn things in ways that relate to him in particular. A time will come when he is more interested in the opinions of his peers in the schoolroom than in those of teachers or parents, but by then he will have already absorbed from his parents the basic principles and values against which he will weigh the influence of his schoolmates. If his identification with his parents is strong, then their moral attitudes will be deeply ingrained. Dr. Erika Freeman says, "If a child is loved and wanted as a human being and related to in a loving way by parents who live according to some ethic, then the child will absorb that ethic." The rub is that too often we find ourselves living without any ethic for the child to absorb.

The young are there waiting for instruction, and we have to teach them *something* if we are to avoid the armies of zonked-out zombies, the walking wounded—directionless, passive, sullen, smug, and ignorant—the advance guard of which is already everywhere around us, sporting signs of the zodiac for religion and "Jesus lives" sweatshirts for amusement, listening to mindless music for mysticism, joining cults and religious communes, staring into vacancy, loving in a void—aging children, pale and wan with mourning for the loss of anything solid in their lives, hungry for something beyond their own concern for self.

Their aimless wandering is really the dark side of their parents' lack of standards. Sheltered for a much longer period of time from those obligations and responsibilities that we assumed at an early age, they have had mothers and fathers afraid to interfere in their teenage lives. The lucky few who were taught that responsibility goes hand in hand with real freedom will exercise that freedom in useful and creative ways; but we see about us all the others who are lost.

Once churches also served as moral preceptors, and parental certainties were reinforced by religious teachings. But churches do not have the influence they once had. When preachers at Pleasant Grove warned us against the evils of dancing or picture shows, we could take them at their word for they were backed up by the authority of the Bible, and the Bible, we believed, was literally true. I remember a man standing in the schoolroom, awkward and ill at ease in his blue workshirt and denim overalls, bringing with him into the room an aura of hard work, of a life spent in intimacy with the earth and growing things, ignorant, earnest, troubled, and touching as he explained to the teacher that he did not want his children to be told again that the world was round. The world was not round. He was certain of it, because though he had no learning, he knew that the Bible tells us to go to the four corners of the earth and preach the gospel to every creature, and the Bible would not have said four corners if there were not four corners, and therefore the world could not be round. He wanted his children to learn to read and write and do figures in their heads, but, please, he did not want to have their faith undermined. The scene is comic in the telling, but his concern and conflict were very real and his pleading eyes and trembling hands were not to be laughed at. And his fear was not unfounded. In being educated, one does get weaned away from the certainties of one's beginnings, and one cannot always be sure that what is gained in the process has more validity than that which is lost.

I would grow away from much that we were taught in that little fundamentalist church, but I cherish the memory of those Sunday mornings, the farmers and their families, clean and combed and dressed in their best, assembling in God's house to celebrate the awesome mystery of creation, to offer up their humility and hope and to reaffirm their resolutions to live in accordance with His law as they understood it. I can still be stirred by memories of the high emotion of revival meetings, though they had their humorous aspects. Maylee Barker would get saved all over again year after year, weeping and screeching, carried finally, limp and fainting, to the altar by her solicitous parents, none of which kept her later on from dying a pathetic death from a self-administered abortion.

I suppose that form of religion was suited to our needs and our sensibilities at that time, and in it we were also taught something of virtue and kindness and pity and compassion that we might not have been able to learn in any other way. But we need more now. Too many churches still threaten hell and damnation to those who don't get on their bandwagon. I do not believe that man can or should be frightened into ethical behavior, and I believe that he is capable of truly miraculous acts of generosity and strength and sacrifice if these are asked of him.

The very words "moral" and "morality" make us uncomfortable because for too long they have been identified with sexual matters. Churches and clergymen used to be preoccupied with sex, and most church training implied that "original sin" and "conceived in sin" had to do with sex. Not so: both doctrines refer to the sinful nature of man, and have nothing to do with conception as a sinful act. For centuries priests and preachers have thundered from their pulpits against pleasure, while the cruelties which man practices on his fellow man have gone virtually unnoted. Our notion of sexual sinfulness owes little to the sweetness, the forgiveness, the compassion of Jesus; it is derived chiefly from the woman-hating, self-hating, and life-hating of the Apostle Paul, who, after some sort of hysterical seizure on the road to Damascus, turned his angry talents from the persecution of Christians to the persecution of the whole world. Ever since Paul, there has been a strong and continuing element of self-torture and hypocrisy in religious teaching, with such influential shouters as Savonarola and Cotton Mather much-admired examples of it at its worst. Significantly, both of those gentlemen heartily endorsed such practices as the burning or the casting out of anyone harboring heretical thoughts, which meant, in effect, anyone who did not wholly agree with them.

I would rather talk of *ethical* considerations, a term which does not suffer from the emotional handicaps surrounding the use of "moral."

I have no quarrel with faith itself, only with the blind, unquestioning acceptance of the forms of religion without a real recognition, examination and experiencing of its content. I do not like religion that values obedience above understanding. We are better off with conflict; as long as we are in conflict, even with ourselves, it means that we are alive, struggling, and that something in us feels, experiences, is trying to assert itself. When Benjamin Franklin said, "In the affairs of this World, Men are saved, not by Faith, but by the Want of it," I very much doubt that he meant to suggest we should ignore the thoughts of Jesus or Buddha or Lao-tzu, but that we must exercise our freedom, seek our own answers. It is in approaching each question with an open mind that we discover, learn, and move forward.

For a time I attended the Meridian Junior College, where a course in World Literature was taught by a splendid little Scotch Presbyterian named Miss Maude Smith. Whenever any subject arose about which any slight controversy was possible, Miss Maude would draw herself up to her full diminutive height and, with a flourish, turn to me. "Mr. Wyatt Cooper," she would say, for all the world like a mischievous angel ushering in the devil, "what is your opinion?" And her eyes would sparkle over her pursed lips while I expounded my unorthodox views (views, mind you, that would hardly qualify as unorthodox elsewhere), accompanied by gasps of amazement and horror from the young Baptist and Methodist maidens in the class. I once asked her why she always called upon me when we were so rarely in agreement. "Because, Mr. Wyatt Cooper, it does those lil' ole girls good to have their narrow little minds shaken up now and then." Her faith, God bless her, was strong enough that she had no fear of my corrupting those lil' ole minds, certainly not so long as she was there to demolish my argument.

It is the search for truth that matters, that transforms, that inspires, not the finding. To question is our principal religious obligation. Those who challenge the authority of God are more likely to serve His purpose than those who worship in servility. Martin Luther said, "I have the right to believe freely. To be a slave to no man's authority. If this be heresy, so be it. It is still the truth. . . . Here I stand. No man can command my conscience." "With what other judgment can I judge but my own?" Joan of Arc asked the Inquisitor and for that presumption she was burned as a heretic, yet she ended up in the calendar of saints.

Beliefs and discoveries and inspirations that once were vital and creative, great leaps of the mind (revelations, if you will), can become codified into empty forms if they are not renewed by fresh insights. Empty forms degenerate into superstition and when this happens, we should be alert to discard them. I have heard people dismiss religion as "fairy tales for children" and in the next breath say they are serious students of astrology. I was, for a time, editor of a magazine, and when I arrived, it carried a column of advice based on the reader's astrological sign. It was written by a secretary who made it up out of her own head, not even consulting any of the numerous books on the subject. I stopped running it, figuring we could put the space to better use, and to my dismay we got many letters from readers complaining that they had been depending on it for daily guidance.

At the same time we must take care that we do not behave like rebellious adolescents and discard along with that which has outlived its purpose much of the spiritual and intellectual tradition that our forefathers have handed down to us. To do so is to embrace an ethical and cultural illiteracy. I do not want my children to grow up knowing or caring nothing for the Psalms of David, the lamentations of Jeremiah, the elegance of Ecclesiastes, the passion of St. Matthew, the defiance of Martin Luther or the strength of Anne Hutchinson. Hard-nosed realism is not a reliable criterion in choosing what we elect to keep. Many of our deepest and most enduring myths have been threatened, but there are truth and power in those myths, great psychological meaning, an expression of man's universal unconscious wisdom. They tell us more about mankind than man knew he knew when he was devising them. They sprang from his need to explain the interaction between himself and his gods, and the themes that occur in those of the simplest tribes are similar to those of the most complex civilizations. To discard myths in favor of some empirical or scientific "truth" is to ignore that capacity for wonder that is so creative a part of man's relationship with the universe. It would be as pointless as to discard science or empiricism for the sake of myth.

To be sidetracked into arguments about whether myths are factually true is, as they say in court, "irrelevant and immaterial." To the ancient Greeks, of course, their stories were a part of what they believed. But suppose there was no young man named Icarus who flew too near the sun; does that make his story any less "real" an expression of man's desire to overleap his limitations? In the same way, must the Ten Commandments have no significance if you don't believe that Moses spoke to a burning bush? The tale of Adam and Eve is beautiful, wise and sublime if read as man's interpretation of his own transition from the innocent child of nature into the knowing, self-aware, striving, judging, and fantasizing creature he became, accountable for his actions. To read it as literal history is to miss the extraordinary truth and splendor of it.

If men invented Jesus, or if fabulous stories grew out of his legend as his influence spread, does that make the Sermon on the Mount a less compelling or less valid affirmation of the humanity of man? The themes of God becoming man, and of man taking on the prerogatives of God, have occurred over and over in religions around the world, and the particular sweetness of Jesus is something that I believe is in us, that, perhaps, evolved in us; it is that most joyful and hopeful assertion that we can rise above ourselves and it comes from our innermost longing for perfection. "Well, yes," Carter said, coming as he usually does to the point ahead of me. "If we made it up, it's even more true, because it's something we feel and not just something that happened to one person."

Religion has given man a sense that his life has meaning, and this is positive; but it has also often encouraged his feelings of dependency. Knowing that he is helpless against the ravages of nature and the tyranny of time, the easy prey of enemies, disease, and events over which he has no control, he has looked to Somebody Up There for succor. God, not himself, was in charge of his life, dispensing punishments and rewards like a severe parent, and the ultimate responsibility for whatever happened, good or bad, was in His hands.

Faith in that kind of deity has declined, but it has not disappeared. For a time it was simply transferred to science. Science and the power of reason became briefly the new religion. There is spectacular beauty in science. It is a splendid monument to the intellect, an indispensable product of the mind of man; and we do well to stand in awe of it. But science is not omnipotent. Its technology is a tool, impersonal and unfeeling, as soulless as its ultimate invention, the computer, which has no eyes, no ears, no heart, no mystery, no wisdom, and no wonder. It knows only what human beings put into it, and it can be no better than those humans who feed it. It has given us weapons but no salvation, means but no ends. The accomplishments of science are sometimes breathtaking, but so are its limitations.

We have also wailed out our woes to the psychoanalysts, and they have sat like German papas at the head of the table and nodded sagely as if they knew, they understood. Like the priests in the confessionals they covered their uncertainties with quotations from the rule books and with silences that were meant to pass for wisdom, and sometimes, like the priests, they have been of help; but they have no divine revelations nor special dispensation from error.

To insist that God or science or our friendly neighborhood alienist must provide us with a meaning for our lives, as if that meaning existed apart from us, is to deny our intrinsic dignity and nobility.

Priests and psychiatrists are recognizing this today, and there is a process of demystification going on. Dr. Carl R. Sonder, New York psychoanalyst, says, "There is an increasing awareness within the profession that real growth takes place when a spirit of collaboration is established between analyst and patient, a relationship that can be characterized as a creative dialogue between equals."

We have come at last to that ultimate point to which the Reformation directed us in which we are our own priests. It has taken this long because though both Luther and Calvin asserted man's right to self-determination, they also had a deep contempt for man and insisted upon his dependency upon God. It begins to dawn on us that after all the millions of years that we have been here, after all that probing and groveling and trying out and boasting and pretending and wondering and cursing and praying, Man has come of age.

As a child grows to maturity, he struggles to liberate himself from the domination of his parents, and suddenly one day he looks around and they are not there. He is faced with the responsibility for his own life. He must live with the blessing and the curse of choice. It is a sobering experience.

We have reached the end of our prolonged puberty and there are no authorities to turn to. God does not intervene. In the midst of his trials, Job was told to curse God and die. We have hurled our blasphemy at the deaf heavens and we do not die. The sun continues to come up as cheerfully as if nobody's hopes had been betrayed. We have acted with a child's conviction that if we protest loudly enough, if we turn ourselves into a public spectacle, someone will come and set things to rights.

But no one comes.

Whether we like it or not, we are free. We are on our own, and now it is up to us.

We do not quite dare believe it, and yet, if we think about it, we have really known it for some time now. It may be that somewhere deep inside our secret selves we knew it all along. All the time we were talking of God and fate and reason and technology, we suspected but dared not breathe aloud that we were talking about ourselves.

Let us pause for a moment, put the *Magnificat* of Bach on the phonograph, and meditate on it for a while.

My life has exactly that meaning, that purpose, and that significance that I give it, that I read into it, that I choose. Apart from what I choose, life has no meaning at all. Apart from what I choose, all else is chance and that design which is imposed by accident, by nature, and by the pattern that has emerged from the process of evolution.

I don't see any call for a new religion. We're always looking for something new, something that arrives fresh and finished, shiny and sparkly-clean like the latest model of an automobile direct from the factory. But we do not require a new set of values. The humanistic tradition is still with us. The Judaeo-Christian concepts of loving our neighbors as ourselves, of being contributing citizens in our communities, are still pretty good guides to follow.

What is needed is that we make them our own. We have to reaffirm them and experience them personally as goals and values that we choose, not as laws that we are forced to follow. Real strength, real integrity, come from living according to the values we truly believe in. In *Man's Search for Himself*, Rollo May puts it this way: "The more profoundly he can confront and experience the accumulated wealth in historical tradition, the more uniquely he can at the same time know and be himself."

Some new perspective won't hurt. A new objectivity, a new subjectivity, a new self-respect, a new starting point. We can begin by saying, Here I am, humble but proud, fearful and anxious but open and willing, and if I can't claim confidence, I can at least claim hope. I stand at the center of my universe. There is only one of me. I have happened only once in all eternity. I refuse to be anonymous. I have a right to my perceptions. And this is what I think I see. This is what I think I know. This is what I think I feel.

"Know thyself," says the Bible. But how? We have been called "hollow men" and we describe ourselves as empty, impotent, apathetic and anesthetized. We are afraid to feel, for our feelings render us vulnerable. But we must get in touch with those feelings. Passion. Pain. Joy. Grief. Anger. Exaltation. We must not run from the emotions that tell us we are alive. We must not tranquilize ourselves with things. Between pain and nothing, I choose pain. We must not move through the extraordinary dramas of our lives like sleepwalkers. An existence that avoids the experiencing of emotion bears the same remote resemblance to life that Muzak bears to Mozart. I once knew an old actress who would press one's hand and whisper with the urgency of one imparting a great secret, "Cherish your sorrow." She had heard the great tragic actress Duse say it. "My dear," she would say, sighing for the greatness that was, "*there* was a woman who knew how to suffer!" We giggled behind her back, of course, but we could do worse than to apply her advice to other emotions as well and try a little cherishing. How sad it is that so many of us have had to seek aid through various of the primal-scream therapies or encounter groups or "touch" systems in order to find out what our feelings are.

"Be yourself," they say, and the first image that comes to my mind is a liberated middle-aged spirit wearing diaphanous veils and prancing around a lawn at twilight, in imitation of those dances of self-expression that were once performed by certain artistic ladies. Then I think of a friend who once said, "Be myself? Are you kidding? If I were ever truly myself for five minutes, you wouldn't stay in the same room with me." But being oneself doesn't mean following every whim or living without controls or censors. It means not being afraid that your true self is so disastrous that people will reject you. It means to be more free, more at ease with your true feelings. Our impulses will still be weighed on the scale of our value judgments, for we have, each of us, some standards that we apply to ourselves. Just be sure they are ours, not somebody else's. We each have a conscience. We will live in peace with ourselves to whatever degree we are able to come to terms with that conscience, and real spontaneity can enrich that peace.

"Get rid of guilt," we've been hearing, and though that is good advice, it needs some qualification. Often we blame ourselves for not being something we have no call to be or for events that are no fault of ours. But in trying to get rid of that excess baggage, there's obviously no point in saying, "I am guilty of nothing." We should feel guilty only of those things of which we *are* guilty. We sometimes use misplaced guilt as a shield behind which we hide genuine guilt, and thereby avoid confrontation with it. If a man abandons his wife and children, I think some sense of guilt would not be out of place for him. Valid guilt is ignored or denied or suppressed at tremendous psychological peril, and no person is mature who avoids responsibility for his acts.

Until recently the prevailing view among psychologists has been that our behavior is determined by conflicting forces in our unconscious, and that which used to be called "free will" (and the will power that we were so often urged to exercise) hardly figured in it. That is a persuasive, even a seductive idea. It suggests that one has no real self, that one's acts are simply the results of inner drives, and it would then follow that one is not to be held responsible for them.

But seductive or not, that is not the way I experience myself. Beyond one's awareness, there is an awareness of one's awareness. I cannot be convinced that there is not a me who, out of that awareness, makes a choice. I cannot be persuaded that I do not in some degree direct myself. I believe that I am capable of affecting myself, of making changes in myself, of affecting others and of making changes in them.

It has been my experience that even at those moments that I am most totally involved, some part of me looks on, takes notes, and comments upon my conduct. This special observer remains largely objective; it retains the detachment, say, of a loving but fair-minded friend. It even has a sense of humor; it is particularly amused by my impulse to cover my insecurity at certain moments by empty posturing or by my attempts, when cornered, to mask my ignorance by bluffing. It laughs most loudly, however, when I suggest to it that perhaps I am, after all, only the tool of my unconscious, and am therefore an innocent. Our unconscious has native wisdom stored away in it; old information and forgotten experiences. What we call intuition often isn't intuition at all, but the stored memory of lessons from our own past. We can contact it and use it, and much of it is rich and rewarding.

Let us learn to feel alive, on a moment-to-moment, day-to-day basis. We've postponed it too long—tomorrow, next year, after this is over, as soon as I've done that, I'll start to live. You are alive now and you are living in this moment. Starting to live is not entering into some new state of existence; it is coming to terms with the one you are in now—whether pleasant or unpleasant, of your own making or imposed from the outside, active or reflective. If you are paying attention to these words, agreeing or disagreeing, gliding over them or using them as springboards for the formation of your own opinions, you are living to whatever degree you are actually involved in the reading. Going to Tahiti next spring may be nice, or taking a course in flower arranging some-day, or starting a new affair when you get the chance, but that is in the future; living is being in touch with what you are doing when you are doing it, even if it is a mundane thing like sweeping the floor. Sweeping the floor is not so onerous a task that you cease to exist while you do it. Doing it well can even be rewarding. If it isn't, then you can use the time to decide what you think about something else. But to suspend your awareness, to close off your thoughts, to erase your attention, is indeed "killing time," surely one of the most distressing of modern phrases.

This morning I was riding in a taxi, and I was using that space of time to try to figure out exactly what I meant by living each moment. My thoughts were distracted by a song on the taxi radio that went something like this: "I drove my Chevy to the levee, but the levee was dry; bye-bye, Miss American Pie . . ." and I listened, wondering why that song gave me an intense pleasure, something akin to the delight I find in certain poems of e.e. cummings. The song ended and the disc jockey came on and asked in the jovial manner of such artists, "Who is going to win our Thanksgiving gobbler today? We have somebody on the line. You have just won our Thanksgiving gobbler, sir. What is your name? The winner, ladies and gentlemen, is Mr. Judas Iscariot from Queens." His name wasn't actually Judas Iscariot; that's only the way I heard it; he spelled it out and it was Julius S. Carriott, but I got out of the taxi glowing with the good feeling that I had just been living a few vivid moments that were worth setting down among my accomplishments for the day.

If asked who we are, by way of reply we name our profession. I am a writer, but that is not who I am. I am a person who is sometimes happy, sometimes not, sometimes confident, sometimes frightened; who enjoys (in carefully disarranged order) books, movies, sex, music, conversation, nature, walking, gardening, thinking, being alone, being in company, being with his family; who hates bad manners, cruelty, rudeness, most card games, Muzak in public elevators, figuring out income tax, looking out of tall buildings, and any conflict or angry confrontation; and who also sometimes writes. Having listed all those things I haven't begun to say who I am. I could say that I am all I remember, the boy weeping on his way to his first day of school, the man looking into his wife's eyes while they waited for their son to be born, a man sometimes tender, sometimes tough, sometimes candid and sometimes deceitful, and still I haven't told it. We grasp at words others use to describe us, as if they will tell us who we are, but words define and limit, and the human personality is vast, deep, mysterious and has no end.

The child begins his life with an eagerness to be everything, to be a part of everything he sees, and his education, too often, becomes a process of closing off, of limitation, of specializing. If he is a good basketball player, that becomes his identity; he might be equally interested in architecture, or in music, but he takes as his own definition that which others see him to be. We have to learn to be less practical. We have to remind ourselves that we can have a passionate interest in something without its having any practical application other than our enjoyment of it. If a child tells us he likes to draw, we immediately ask him if he wants to be an artist when he grows up, or, perhaps, if we are *really* practical-minded, we tell him that artists starve to death, as if his interest were useless unless he planned to use it in some utilitarian way, ignoring the richness it brings into his life now, dismissing its "usefulness" in expressing his feelings about the world around him or the delight he takes in form and color. We mustn't mind being amateurs, and we must not surrender those things that give us real pleasure just because we can't make a living from them.

We can play tennis without being champions, enjoy carpentry for its own sake, plumbing for pleasure.

Which brings us to the matter of competition, the obligation of winning, of proving ourselves, of seeing ourselves in terms of two possible roles—as victor or as vanquished. It has a long and honorable history, that spirit of competition, and it has been responsible for much of the real progress that has taken place in the past few centuries. It sprang from that emphasis on individuality and individual achievement that began with the flowering of the Renaissance, and without it there would not have been the explosion of the industrial age, the amazing series of discoveries, inventions, and experimentation that have made our lives more comfortable and more fruitful, and that have widened so astonishingly the range of our potentialities. But in our time we have retained the manner, the style, and the negative aspects of competition without the sense of real accomplishment or sense of purpose that must once have made it meaningful.

We have assumed that the drive to dominate, to control, to act aggressively toward our fellow men, was inherent in our makeup. Certainly I never doubted it. There was evidence enough in the schoolyard. "I can beat you up," one boy would say to another by way of making conversation. I can even remember, in desperation, finding someone weaker than myself to whom I could say it to preserve some grain of self-respect, to prove to myself that if I was not as tough as Wallace Hamburg (which I clearly was not; his claim went undisputed in my set, and we lined ourselves up accordingly, though we could not then know that he would die as a murderer a few years later in the electric chair), I could at least assert my minor claim elsewhere. I suspect that many creative people, intellectuals, moralists, philosophers, clergymen, live with the secret fear that the shape of their lives, the form of their striving toward expression, is all based on compensating for their physical cowardice, the feeling that if only they'd proved themselves on the football team, or even by a willingness to fight in the schoolyard, it would be worth more than all the prizes that they may have won elsewhere.

In our personal lives that artificial assertion of potency, that obligation to effect a series of daily victories, has created an atmosphere of hostility and suspicion among us. How can men work together toward common goals when their inner conviction is that they must each advance at a co-worker's expense? It makes for false relationships, empty postures, and phony bravura. But I believe this is changing. It seems to me that we are becoming more relaxed with each other. The women's movement has given even to those women who are not actually a part of it a new sense of sisterhood. Men talk about it less, but unless I'm fooling myself, I see a new openness in their encounters too. I used to have the impression that many men on social occasions, the moment the women retired to another room and cigars were brought out, would begin circling each other like wary animals, watching for the first sign of bared teeth. Conversations were guarded, cautious, determinedly impersonal and lacking in spontaneity or pleasure. Discussions often became arguments as if the only purpose of talking was to score a point over an opponent. I sense, these days, a new willingness to share experiences, points of view, even feelings.

That same fear and suspicion have been a part of our love relationships. Those whom we would love become threats if we fear that the feeling we have for them will somehow expose our vulnerability; to admit our feeling for the beloved is to indicate weakness. The sex act then becomes a challenge, the bed a testing ground, another crisis to be overcome; and we approach it with apprehension lest we fail to measure up. Our partners become enemies to be conquered, or strangers to be dominated, impersonal and unidentified embodiments of what we fear in ourselves. In such a climate the longing for physical, mental, and spiritual communication, the mutual exploration of feeling and response, the relaxation of being open to experience, the release that comes in accepting one's vulnerability, the sheer delight of taking and giving pleasure, the closeness, the warmth, the tender, timeless other-worldness of it, the real joy and beauty of the sexual gift, are simply missed for the sake of conquest. The sex clinics, the manuals, the preoccupation with technique, the swinging couples, the crossing over, the dismissal of old taboos, old concepts of the norm—all this is, I think, the clamor that accompanies change. Behind it, something important seems to be happening: a new appreciation of a vital part of ourselves, a refusal to settle for less, which is not unrelated to the similar sort of breakthrough that is taking place in the redefining of our sex roles. Out of it, with any luck, should come a better respect for ourselves and for each other. Once we as men and women get beyond our bitterness about the past, the recriminations and accusations that grew out of mutual misunderstandings, we should realize that we're all in this together, and we should be able to settle down into some calm acceptance of our freedom.

11

Where Do We Go from Here?

"The future is purchased by the present."
—Samuel Johnson

What, then, is the future of the family? That is the question I am most often asked by those who know of my interest in the subject. I have found that the young, who are still trying to decide what shape they want their lives to take, are as concerned about it as the old.

One thing that seems to have altered permanently is the expectation that everyone should produce children. The fear of an overpopulated world has taken care of that. We may soon begin to worry that the birth rate is declining where it shouldn't decline rather than where it should, but that is for the future to decide. In the past, there has been tremendous pressure, especially on young women, exerted by friends, family, and society alike, that they get married, and once married, that they bear children. If a woman did not do either or both, she was made to feel that she was somehow betraying life's purpose for her, and that there was some major flaw in her character. We heard a great deal in those days about the maternal instinct, and any woman who had the gall to admit openly that she didn't want children was looked upon as being almost as freakish as she would have been if she'd announced that she had been born without sex organs. The childless couple was looked upon with pity. All that has changed. God knows it has changed. Pregnancies are often greeted with surprise if not outright disapproval. Many women used to have children because their mothers urged it, their husbands took it for granted, society demanded it, or their birth control method failed them. Today we realize that not every woman has a maternal instinct any more than all men desire to be fathers. Those women who have no relish for motherhood should suffer no criticism and should feel no guilt about their attitude.

Psychiatrists' waiting rooms, hospital wards, juvenile courts, and prisons overflow with the offspring of unwilling parents. For a mother to give birth to an unwanted child is to do an injustice to herself, to the child, and to the world at large. Babies have a right to be wanted, to be welcomed. The child forms an idea of his role in the world, a beginning sense of his own identity, that depends upon whether he feels treasured and cherished or neglected, disliked, or simply an object of indifference. The unwanted children who are made to feel that they are in the way, the children who are told or made to feel that they are "bad," will be, eventually, turned loose like a plague upon the world, to spend their lives wreaking havoc upon those around them. Some will be able to hold responsible positions and to form families of their own, but they will remain unformed, angry, resentful, and suspicious; they will trust neither themselves nor anyone else; and they will give to their own children a legacy of hurt and horror that can be passed on from generation to generation, handed down like heirlooms, until somebody has the will or the luck to find the strength to break the chain.

It is to be hoped that in the future only those will bear children who burn with an uncommon devotion to the family, couples who see themselves as joining hands with the Creator in bringing forth life. There are many who do feel something like that, and it may be that an aptitude for parenting is a talent like any other. It is to be hoped that if the day comes when a legal limit is set on the number of children parents are allowed to bear, exceptions will be made for those who share that passion for parenthood, for the children of such unions are likely to be a blessing to the communities they enter. There are women who do not feel trapped in the home, who do not feel that they are wasting their lives and betraying their potential by spending the early years at home with their young, though some are becoming embarrassed to say so. They should not be made to feel any more apologetic for that desire than should those of their sisters who feel more alive in the world of work. Nor need the two worlds be exclusive, one of the other. We know that it isn't the quantity of time spent with the children that matters, but the quality. I have sometimes been distressed to read accounts of those women who felt demeaned by the time and effort they spent looking after their children. I'm not talking about housework, or being a domestic drudge—that's another matter. It seems to me that for those who do enjoy children, nothing else in their lives will ever be as fulfilling as those early years with them, nothing as challenging as the responsibility for what goes into those little heads. I am speaking not as an outside observer looking on but as a father who has been at home with his children most of the time. Many fathers, these days, are discovering the joy of participating in the upbringing of their children. To be sure, my situation was not the same as that of overworked mothers who are stuck with being chauffeurs, cooks, dishwashers, and general handymen, and whose efforts have often gone unappreciated. I was not tied to the house; I did not have to do washing or cleaning up; I had a wife, nurse, and others who participated, so that I really had the best of it. I had time to myself: I could get on with my work and I could choose the length and the nature of my time with the children, but, still, I found an excitement and a joy that I have never experienced elsewhere.

Emerson once said that love is like a mathematical equation:

you get out of it what you put into it. I don't know if that is always true, but I am certain that with children what you put in you get back tenfold. Too many fathers, busy with careers or preoccupied with providing the neccessities of food and shelter, have paid little attention to their children during the earlier years. The feeling has been that it is women's work and that fathers are not equipped for it. Many men are uncomfortable with infants and do not really get to know their children as the individuals they are until they are old enough to be young persons demanding their slice of time. This is regrettable, both because the father misses one of the meaningful experiences of a lifetime and because something important is lacking in the life of the child. The father brings the outside world to the child. Particularly is this true for boys. Many boys live only with women in a women's world in the first few years, and the father's bulk, strength, deep voice, and general hairiness can seem foreign and frightening, a creature very different from himself. Once my sons and I were in the elevator setting out on some jaunt when Anderson was just beginning to form sentences. "Are Mommy and May going?" he asked. "No," I answered, "only the men." He blinked. "The men?" he asked, leaning his head back to look up the miles of space between his face and mine. "Yes," I said, "the men. You and Carter and me." "Oh," he said. He straightened out his head, lifted his tiny shoulders. A grin of smug satisfaction spread across his face and we rode down the rest of the way in thoughtful silence.

Many suggestions are now being made for alternative ways of forming families. Communes are springing up and some suggest them as a new form of family life. Certainly the modern ones have come into existence not so much as communities in which particular ideas or ideals could be put into practice (like the Transcendentalists in the nineteenth century), but more in response to a deeply felt need for some sort of clan life broader than that of the tight, small, and socially isolated family. One benefit, when children are involved, and for those adults seeking to readjust to the lacks in their childhoods, is the presence of surrogate fathers and mothers, a sense of oneself as a part of a larger group; but generally such communes are molded around the personality of one strong person who sets the style, and when he fails or moves on, the newfound family becomes centerless and is dissolved. Those seeking an extended marriage usually find that what has failed for two can as readily fail for a dozen.

Others are trying to extend their families in informal ways, without sharing income, sex, or domiciles. There is a movement in many Unitarian churches to form associations in which couples, young or old, with or without children, single parents, grandparents—people from almost any domestic situation—join together for weekends, holidays, or other occasions, keep in touch with each other, rally around when sickness or trouble arises, and behave, in general, such as any blood-related family might.

Some envision state-supported day care centers, with considerable expansion of their services, or group homes patterned, perhaps, after the Israeli kibbutzim, with children from unsettled family situations brought together, trained, and looked after in a constructive, enlightened, and supportive environment, with visits from parents but with the group itself remaining the stable center of the children's lives, and this seems to me to be a field deserving of study and experimentation. In Israel, the kibbutzim, of course, benefit from a very special circumstance; that is, the parents are themselves highly motivated people and their relationship with their children is strong and personal. These are not rejected or unloved offspring. There is no parental abandonment of responsibility or lack of involvement with their children. Whether such a project could meet with much success among the urban poor remains to be seen, but clearly there are possibilities here that should not be ignored.

There is no end of suggestions, but when you come down to

it, the essence of the family is one man and one woman, their love for each other, and the children who grow out of that love, and there has never been any other really satisfactory system for bringing up children. We must take into some account that the needs of the human child are not simply those of food, shelter, and protection from marauders. His mind and heart must be nurtured if he is to become a rational, functioning, contributing member of our complex society. It is only in quite recent times that we have taken to overromanticizing the family; and, perhaps we have placed too heavy a burden of expectation upon it, a burden that is unfair in today's restrictive circumstances. But I do not honestly see it that way. I believe that it is suffering mainly from the pull of the outside world, from the multiplicity of alternatives available to its members, and from that lack of solid personal identity that affects almost everyone in our society. As families grew smaller, the participants in each family fewer, and the responsibility for its preservation concentrated upon those few, it happened that there was, at the same time, a shrinking of the individual's feelings of confidence, capability, and potency. But it is possible that the clear and present danger to the family, a threat that we all recognize, may be the very force that will in the end draw us together in its defense. In any case, I do not, myself, see any real alternative. Visions of test-tube infants being raised in laboratories and brought up by specialists make interesting reading in the Sunday supplements, but they will remain just that—visions. In the first place, we might well ask "Why?" What would they be raised for? If life became as impersonal and without human need or human warmth as that, I don't see why anyone would want to live it. In the second place, it is impossible to raise children in pots, like geraniums lined up in a hothouse. Without human nurturing they simply die.

The question of the family's future was asked recently by Nadine Brozan in an article in the *New York Times*, and the consensus of replies, from the sociologists, anthropologists, psychiatrists, and theologians she questioned was that it is sorely threatened, it is surely changing, but that it shows every evidence of surviving. Professor Amitai Etzioni, professor of sociology at Columbia, was quoted: "If I had to predict—and I do so with great reluctance —I think the time is ripe for a great resurrection of the American family, and I think that people will start romanticizing marriage. . . . They're getting tired of freewheeling attitudes and they're threatened by the removal of taboos. There is great insecurity caused by the fact that anybody can walk out at any moment, and people are searching for new, positive definitions." Dr. Benjamin Spock has said, ". . . Obviously the family is changing and a lot of that change is to the good. Most people who don't want a legal commitment are openly living together, and that's fine as long as there are no children . . . and some are marrying but don't want children, and that's fine, too. Only those people who can't resist children should have them; there's no practical reason ever to have children."

The success of the individual family and of the family as an institution will depend upon the maturity we achieve individually and as a people.

We have to re-examine love. Really examine it. We've heard so much about it, read so much, sung so much, said so much, that the very word means nothing, and one's almost ashamed to bring it up. It's the four letters on a pop art postage stamp that we stick on an envelope to the butcher. All the movies we've ever been to have been about love—young love, cute love, true love, blue love —it's been sprayed about our living like Airwick; it's been droned into us that Love Is All. Love conquers. Happily ever after. We'll fall in love and it'll be Ginger Rogers and Fred Astaire dancing down to Rio.

One is tempted to say it's all lies, but that's not true. It's not all lies. Falling in love is everything they say it is. It *is* the sun in the morning and the moon at night and walking on clouds and singing in the rain. Falling in love *is* wonderful, and the only thing is that it has no relation to loving. Well, yes, it has; to be accurate, we must admit that there is a relation, but loving is something that happens later on, afterward, when all the songs have died away, the fireworks have been displayed, and the alluring, mysterious enigma of the flesh has become the familiar, the known, the cherished. Romantic love is an itch in the bloodstream, and if you work it right, you can keep it in constant agitation. Falling in love is so easy a thing that some can and do accomplish it with every change of the moon. Romantic love is rapture, a yearning for the infinite, and it's fine exercise for the hurried heart and the fleet of foot, but taking that and making it grow into something deeper and richer is a lot of trouble, and should not, I suppose, be too readily embarked upon by the restless and impatient or those seeking after uninterrupted ecstasy.

For the real thing lies in the tender afterglow; it is in the everyday concern for another's welfare; it is in the quiet and deep and safe wonder that the beloved is there, that the beloved's life is touched by you, nourished by you; it is in giving the best of yourself; and the depth and breadth of it, its polyphonic beauty, come almost as a surprise, as an afterthought, as peace after passion; it is to be felt in solitude as well as in the presence.

Marriage used to be considered a sacrament, and if there is to be true love in it, there should be some element akin to religious devotion, a kind of dedication to a concept larger than ourselves, more important than our daily wants.

But we aren't talking about marriage here. Like everything else, marriage has changed. The demands on it have been severe. We've found out we aren't Ginger and Fred. We're a generation with a great sense of outrage that nothing has been what they told us it was. We've based our hopes on the cute meetings and the

funny quarrels of Cary Grant and Katharine Hepburn, and, somehow, our partners do not seem to have seen the same movies.
They don't make the right replies, and the mornings after are not
as adorable as we'd been led to believe. Our fantasy lives have not
prepared us for flat eggs, bad coffee, or disgruntled breakfast
partners with tousled hair.

Previous generations anticipated less and got more. Our grandparents did not expect and were not expected to understand each
other, to spend time sharing sensitive and intimate thoughts or
looking deep into each other's being; they had things to do; he
did what he did and she did what she did and when night came
they did what they did and then went off to sleep without the
troubling feeling that they'd missed out on a meaningful relationship. But we have brought to marriage the bewildering cargo of
our needs and our lacks and our absence of real identity, and now
everybody says it has failed, so marriage is changing. Ceremonies
are being dropped, legalities neglected, and the rites of passage
in and out of it are much easier all around. And that's all right
too. So long as marriage is meant for two, it's the concern of those
two and nobody else, really. Whether it is with or without clergy,
whether it lasts a weekend or a lifetime, is really their affair.

So it's not marriage we're concerned about here, but the family,
and this is a field that requires a more blessed climate and a fuller
season. If two people are going to take on the prerogatives of the
Maker and create new life, then there'd better be some kind of
sacrament somewhere in the transaction. Children need a mother
and they need a father, and it takes a lot of years to get them
where they're going, so one must proceed with some caution. One
must be prepared to make some commitment, and if it seems too
heavy a load to carry, then it is not for you.

When I was young, divorce was considered a tragedy. Today
it is commonplace. So long as it is a solution for ending a soured
relationship between two people it is a godsend, and the hypocriti-

cal way that it is treated legally is a farce. It is astonishing that there are still states and courts that continue the fiction that there must be a guilty party and a (presumably) injured one. This is a vindictive inheritance from canon law; it has no relation to the truth of human nature; it is out of touch with present realities, and it benefits no one but the lawyers who profit from it. Two people enter voluntarily into a partnership, and, so long as no one else's welfare is concerned, they should be able to withdraw mutually from that partnership just as voluntarily. But marriage between two people is one thing and marriage with children is another, a difference that is not taken into proper account today. When a family is dissolved, it is a matter of three, four, five, or more people being divorced, and the secondary partners in the proceeding are casually disposed of like so much property, or used by the principals as weapons against each other. Just as the giving of life to children should be a sacred matter, so should be the matter of their dispersal, and in the most civilized of separations, even with the most considerate kind of planning, it is, for the children involved, except in cases where the departing parent has been destructive to them, nothing less than tragedy.

Obviously, if the tension at home is insufferable, the children will be damaged by it, and there is some point at which repair becomes impossible and it is better for all concerned that a break occur; but there is no way to avoid the glaring fact that the parent who moves out—almost always the father—is, however liberal his "visitation" rights, cut off from any really effective participation in the upbringing of the children. They will interpret his absence as an abandonment, and they will lack the influence of his presence in the home.

"Growth" is a familiar word these days. It's very big among the popular advisers to the restless. Any sly puss who writes a book giving us a new, fanciful, and sincere-sounding way of justifying "I'm out for me, Old Number One" is bound to do well in the marketplace and be hailed as a prophet into the bargain. Whenever any phenomenon is as widespread as divorce has become, there will arise an eager host of opportunists to cash in on the anxieties connected with it. Any married couple, after spending a few evenings with the current crop of books on the creativity of divorce, can only begin to feel that in staying together they are stifling not only their own growth but that of their children. I think of a remark made by a lady of my acquaintance concerning her ex-husband, who was a psychiatrist. "My God," she said, "when I think that that man is in charge of people's minds!" It seems to fit in here.

Making a change is not quite the same thing as growth, is it? If it were, we'd all be giants by now.

If someone wants to switch partners every other season, it's all right with me. I just don't want to hear about what "growth" it was each time.

Well, enough of that. Fads come and go, and this, too, will pass.

We must dare to set high aims for ourselves. We must stop proclaiming our limitations, stop announcing the names of our weaknesses and using those names as justification for becoming no better. We can rise above ourselves. We must rise above ourselves.

12

---··⟨∾∾⟩··---

In Conclusion

We that acquaint ourselves with every zone
And pass both tropics and behold the poles,
When we come home are to ourselves unknown,
And unacquainted still with our own souls.
— JOHN DAVIES, *"Nosce Teipsum"*

What a chimera, then, is man! What a novelty! What
a monster, what a chaos, what a contradiction, what
a prodigy! Judge of all things, feeble worm of the earth,
depository of truth, a sink of uncertainty and error, the
glory and the shame of the Universe. — PASCAL

This book came about because of an essay I wrote on the meaning of the family for the Christmas, 1973, issue of *Town & Country* magazine. In the months following its appearance I received an astonishing number of letters from readers. Most came from those who were concerned about the future of the family. Many wrote about their own troubled family situations. Others wrote asking, "What can we do? What can I do?" "We know what the problems are," one lady wrote. "What we need are solutions."

Obviously, she is right. I don't know whether I have any solutions to offer, or even whether there are any real solutions as such. In this book I have written primarily about my own experiences and my own feelings, because all one really knows, in the end, is what one has oneself experienced and felt, and all one can offer

186

is to share something of one's passion for life.

It may be that the best thing we can do for our families is to see that we are ourselves living in some harmony with life. There is so much that is beyond our control. Our children go out into a world where they are influenced by other people, shaped by events that are not of our making, influenced by cultural attitudes that we may neither approve of nor understand. We cannot and should not live their lives for them, any more than we can for our brothers, sisters, wives, or husbands. We cannot alter the world, and we are powerless to resist the shifting currents of our times. Sometimes, all we can do is see that our own lives are in order.

Some years ago I was a guest in the house of a very old lady. One morning I came down to breakfast to find her sitting by the window, her hair still in long braids from the night, having tea with her nurse-companion. "How do you feel?" I asked. Quickly, with a child's toss of the head, and in a singsong voice, she shot back, "With my fingers." Startled by her own reply, she stared at me for a moment, and then began to sob. I tried to console her, but she would not be comforted. "It was a childish thing to say," she kept repeating, while I tried to assure her that it was not. "Come now," I said, "why are you crying?" She lifted her head with some defiance and answered firmly, "I am crying because I am old and I don't want to die."

I think of her often. I think of that statement, flat and unvarnished, strung out between us in the room like icicles hanging from a line, and I can feel again the deadly chill of truth that froze us both into silence.

Well, we are born old and we are all of us dying, and it is imperative that before it is too late we learn, for the sake of the tomorrows remaining, to cherish this incredible gift of life that is ours.

We are always being told that, and it's easy enough to say "Go out and live" as if we were addressing the three little pigs as they set out in the world to seek their fortunes. In joining the chorus, I don't know that we are passing on anything that is of any help to those asking "How?" How do we, at this late date, start learning how to live? We all want to live. None of us wants to choose death; we don't even want to walk around as we now do, seething with anger. How then?

It should be understood that when I say "live" I am not speaking for the adoption of some hedonistic life style or the seeking of instant gratification for every impulse. Those who deliberately embark on that "hell-bent on having a good time" sort of thing usually end up alone and fat, weeping onto their own distorted images in glasses of champagne gone flat. Setting out on an orgy of self-gratification and pleasure-seeking is far too hysterical an approach for real assurance.

We might start by getting a little better acquainted with ourselves. Introduce yourself to yourself, and then accept that self. It is a process, not an event, and it will take time. Take a little private inventory of what really works in your life and what doesn't. Do it several times and take a bigger slice of honesty each time. What do you really feel? Believe? Want? Avoid striking poses. Don't decide the result in advance and then make your examination a matter of finding evidence that will fit the mold. Look at the beauty around you. I don't mean just the glow of sunsets. More than that. Examine the beauty of people: the beauty of their minds, their complexity, their vulnerability, the puzzle of them. Start from scratch, and don't be inhibited by thinking you're going to have to *act* on what you find. Suppose, to take a trivial example, you decide that you don't really like your best friend; you've never really liked him or his jokes or his wife, and yet you've spent twenty years' worth of Friday nights playing Chinese checkers with the two of them, simply because they were there and *they* called you. The main thing is to admit to yourself that you don't like him. Once you've admitted that, you don't even have to stop the checker games; you may even begin to enjoy them without having to get drunk first. Or suppose you have one of those mothers who's collapsing into senility without ever pausing in her long recitation of how much she's sacrificing for you. Once you stop punishing yourself by agreeing with her in your own mind, and once you stop reprimanding yourself for not being more worthy of her nobility, once you do that, you don't even have to get rid of her. You can sit patiently while she rattles on and on; you can even feel sorry that she needs to reassure herself in that way.

Being honest with yourself does not mean that you're going to throw responsibility aside, desert your spouse and children, and elope with the new file clerk at the office. This should not be taken as an excuse for irresponsibility. One of the arguments I have with psychological therapy and with many of those "discover yourself" books is that they often encourage what seems to me to be a monstrous selfishness, disregarding our very human need to be of help to others, to feel that our life has some beneficial effect upon those whose lives touch ours. In fact, you may find that what you need most is to feel useful. There is nothing more essential to the healthy human spirit. If your wife has long since ceased to value your opinions, if your children will have none of your counsel, if the other fellows at the office wouldn't dream of confiding in you with their problems, if all your acquaintances take on that glazed look when you start outlining your plans for the new world order, then find something or somebody to whom you can be of use. Pick a good cause to work for, preferably one where you can see the direct result of your action.

Rediscover people. Notice those you have been seeing every day without really seeing them. Talk to people outside your regular circle, people in worlds different from yours. Re-examine the relationships that exist. Perhaps you haven't really appreciated the worth, the complexity, the needs of those you live with. Take nothing for granted.

Learn to be a little satisfied with your status and your place; at least, do so if you have no way out of that place. We are bound to the notion that every man can become a king, or at least a tycoon, and with the notion that every man should *want* to be a king, which is an uncertain notion to begin with. I don't mean, of course, that one should live contentedly in poverty, or accept the role of second-class citizen; I only mean that there is dignity in all constructive work, and one's opinion of oneself should not come from where one ranks in the social order. The plumber or the bus driver or the schoolteacher sometimes feels or is made to feel that his profession is a badge of shame, and, accordingly, he takes no pride in doing it well, or in doing it at all. We have to learn that we are under no obligation to be anything other than the person we are.

Along with the dissatisfaction with what one has accomplished goes the sad conviction that all those others out there somehow have had it easy. This feeling is by no means limited to what used to be called the lower orders. I'm sure that many a company head, if you took him aside for a drink and gave him a long sympathetic look, would explain how uneasy sits the head that wears a crown, and how he envies the humble porter who can lie abed of a night without a care in the world. Anybody who has lived abroad can tell you of having known happy carpenters, happy salesmen, happy domestics, happy lords and ladies, and happy peasants in other countries; there are those who have found contentment wherever they are on the pile. We must figure out how they did it. We don't have to live without ambition, but we do have to live within our capabilities and with our own expectations, not those expectations imposed upon us by an aggressive society.

Simplify. If you've taken on too much, pare it down. If there are too many social demands, decide which ones you really want. Be unavailable. The world won't fall apart. Be selfish when the call upon your time, talent, and attention is not useful, and un-selfish when you are really needed. Both are a part of living.

We must learn again to be joyous. We needn't be ashamed of our small vanities or little follies, our infatuation with the fripperies of life. Those things are a part of what we are, part of the charm and the paradox of man. That we seek to embellish our lives with some attempt at decoration, that we have a notion of beauty, an idea of grace, is surely more than fancy icing on a cake of corruption. It is some sign of a kind of maturing of the human spirit. It is an expression of our hunger for balance and proportion, our need to make order out of confusion. We are a perceptive and responsive animal, and in that perception and in that response we come close to creation itself. When man thrills to the grandeur of the heavens and to the splendor in the flower, he partakes of that grandeur and of that splendor.

We must rediscover the healing gift of laughter. Christopher Fry has said, "Laughter is the surest touch of genius in creation. Would you ever have thought of it, I ask you, if you had been making man, stuffing him full of such hopping greeds and passions that he has to blow himself to pieces as often as he conveniently can manage it—would it also have occurred to you to make him burst himself with such a phenomenon as cachinnation? That same laughter, madam, is an irrelevancy which almost amounts to revelation."

Real laughter starts down deep in the belly and rises up through all the organs and comes out of the mouth a pleasure and a relaxation, almost as satisfying as sex. It's a healthy bellow that comes from seeing the folly and the fun of human endeavor. William Hazlitt said, "Man is the only animal that laughs and weeps; for he is the only animal that is struck with the difference between what things are, and what they ought to be."

Even the sound of laughter has changed. It no longer can be said to "ring out." People whinny or they snort, trying to hold it in so that it comes out in apologetic little hacks. They feel somehow that it's a social offense to laugh. How long has it been since you heard it said of somebody that his laughter made you feel good? Does anybody any longer have an infectious laugh? Why, I remember from my youth that when Louise Long used to laugh you could hear her half a mile away, and you would pause in your occupation to smile to yourself. Laughter traveled in those days; it went through the woods, past the graveyard, and across the fields, and it was always like the sun breaking through the clouds.

We have to learn to look at things and know that they are funny. Actually, we have to discover all over again how to enjoy. Enjoyment is almost as extinct as the horse and buggy. One goes to the theatre to keep up with Joneses and to the movies to be educated, and one plays golf in order to get a new account for the agency. Many of us actually feel guilty about pleasure of any sort if it's pleasure for its own sake. Catch a man "just hacking around" and see if he doesn't apologize. How many people have the courage to doze off on the floor on Sunday morning with the unread monument of the *New York Times* scattered around them? No, they must drive themselves on and on through the canyons of the newspaper in order to feel that they're doing their duty, and even then there's so much of it left unexamined that they feel they are cheating if they pass on to something else.

We've got to make up our minds that we deserve a good time, after all. Forgive yourself, already. You've spent more than your time in purgatory. We've got to forgive ourselves our trespasses better than we've been forgiving those who've trespassed against us. And in this matter of forgiving it's not so much our trespasses that I worry about. Actually, I think our trespasses have got to be faced, and that squarely. Those cruelties we've committed and the kindnesses we've left uncommitted have got to be confronted, and then taken care of. We avoid dealing with them by wallowing in a great deal of masochistic guilt about other irrelevant things. Like thoughts. Because our wilder thoughts frighten us, we quickly spank ourselves and turn off our imagination. Look, everybody has these wicked thoughts; everybody has a momentary wish that he could successfully embezzle a few thousands, or see all his enemies dead at his feet, or possess his neighbor's wife, and what they do, those thoughts, is let off steam. The late Theodor Reik said, "No one should ever have a guilt feeling about his thoughts. If you stand before Tiffany's window and want to steal some of its contents, there's no reason for a guilt feeling. The more guilty your thoughts make you feel the more likely you are to commit a crime."

We've got to learn how to get up in the morning and look at the sky (or at least at the glimpse we can still get of it now and then), breathe air into our lungs (no comment), look about us at what is good, gaze into a fresh flower, sink into an infant's smile, listen to the music when someone says, "Good morning," and means it. We must *enjoy!* The day will soon come when we'll be old and not wanting to die, and it'll be a lot easier if we can look back on a life that had its share of the delight that was its rightful portion.

Throughout the ages Man has been obsessed with himself. He has glorified himself and he has castigated himself. The greatest minds among men have tried to define him. "Man is a biped without feathers," said Plato. "Man is the measure of all things," said Protagoras. Shakespeare said, "Is man no more than this? Consider him well . . . a poor, bare, forked animal." Aldous Huxley said, "Man is an intelligence in servitude to his organs." Pascal said, "Man is but a reed, the most feeble thing in nature, but he is a thinking reed." Alexander Pope called him "a being darkly wise and rudely great," and George Chapman said, "Man is a name of honour for a king." We used to stand up in church and sing, from the great old hymn "From Greenland's Icy Mountains," ". . . though every prospect pleases, and only man is vile."

Poor man; what is he to think of himself in all this? One minute he's told he's created in God's image; the next minute he's told (by Mark Twain) that of all the animals, he's the only one who blushes, or needs to.

We have learned an astonishing lot about the nature of man the beast in the last half-century or so, and nobody rejoices in this knowledge more than I do. The relatively new science of psychology has informed us about the unbridled motives of our animal nature; we recognize our crimes and cruelties, and our raging lusts and passions do not go unnoted. The practitioners of that science have unlocked many mysteries of the human mind and shown us things undreamed of before our time. (Except, of course, by the poets; they knew it all along. Aeschylus knew. So did Sophocles, Shakespeare, Dante, others; but that's another story.) Much of the cruel destruction of which we are capable has been brutally underlined for us by events. We have seen the monstrous and inhuman acts that man performed in Germany; we have seen such acts in Africa, and we have seen them here at home. It is a central fact of our time: a revelation to us that in this enlightened age a people not unlike ourselves sat by and looked on, or looked the other way, or participated, in the cold, deliberate slaughter of millions of their fellow citizens. It told us something about ourselves that we must live with forever.

But an odd thing has happened; we've come rather to take a perverse pleasure in the ugly vision of ourselves, as if the recognition absolved us of responsibility. When we listen to what is being said around us, we begin to feel that all human effort is suspect, that there really is no such thing as dignity, or compassion, or any of those other qualities of the human heart that the best of men have treasured and nourished all these long centuries since we came down from the trees and began improving our manners. It would seem that beauty is nothing more than an illusion, truth a fallacy, and nobility a trick of the light.

Well, I wouldn't want anybody to forget the lessons we have learned at such cost, but I do think it is imperative, if we are to grow into anything at all, that we remind ourselves from time to time that man is himself something of a miracle, and that he is capable of the miraculous. As a race and as individuals, we have accomplished incredible things. We are blessed with judgment and we can make choices. You and I are each capable of kind feelings and good deeds. We have even, on occasion, felt those feelings and performed those deeds.

Man learned to reason. He invented language and an alphabet and he has built libraries to store his accumulated wisdom for the ages. He searched for ways to relieve pain and he has found them. He has been capable of courage and sacrifice and nobility of mind and splendor of spirit. He built the Parthenon, the Sistine Chapel, the Taj Mahal, and the Golden Gate Bridge. He wrote *Oedipus Rex* and *King Lear* and the Bible; he has composed great symphonies that speak to some special region of the soul beyond words and logic and definition. He discovered fire and the wheel and penicillin and how to form various styles of government that have often managed to work well enough for most practical purposes.

There is something of God in us after all; somewhere along the line of our evolution there was born into our race (or it was breathed into Adam if you prefer a more literal interpretation of our beginnings) the wild promise of wisdom, and if we forget that, it may cease to exist in us. There is in all of us and each of us, the mightiest and the lowest, always the possibility of the miracle. Each of us has the divine gift of reason and the incredible, unfathomable wonder of life. We must cherish it in ourselves and in each other.

Shakespeare marveled at man and he despaired of him. He has Hamlet say:

What a piece of work is a man! how noble in reason! how infinite in faculties! in form and moving, how express and admirable! in action, how like an angel! in apprehension, how like a god; the beauty of the world! the paragon of animals! And yet, to me, what is this quintessence of dust? Man delights not me. . . .

If we are to survive, Man *must* delight us. We must somehow find our way to the notion that Man *is* desirable. The time has come, I think, that we say a few words in praise of ourselves. It is time to speak once again of the genius of mankind. Man, with his puny little body, his puny little mind, and his puny little conscience, has, with his puny little voice, talked himself into being better than he perhaps had any reason to expect himself to be. We must not now let him talk himself out of it again.

There are those who swear that meanness is built into us. They say that man is a cheat and a liar, a sneak and a thief, a selfish beast who takes what he wants, destroys what he cannot use, and leaves a trail of waste behind him; and we have, each of us in our lifetimes, seen some indication of truth in this. But I also believe in his heroism. He is a plucky fellow with surprises up his sleeve, and I find him likable. He has his dreams, he lives with his visions, and a part of his tragedy is that he judges himself against the splendor of those dreams and visions. In the face of terrible odds he keeps plugging away. He finds himself pitted against the sly tricks of his fellows, the yapping disasters of nature, the sabotage of his own inner conflicts even; and yet, like a battered old alley cat, he comes through, a bit torn but tougher for the fray, swaggering still, and facing the survivors' world with a grin and a giggle. Somebody has said that we are fragile creatures, abandoned by an indifferent universe, cast adrift in a frail craft on a troubled sea with little more than a broken compass to guide us —a broken compass, plus some small knowledge of the stars, a tribal memory of past escapes, and the deep, burning, and abiding will to live. We are buffeted about, from within and without, and we manage miraculously to survive for a time.

In that long march from our beginnings we have often faced disaster, and from somewhere within us some determination to live has asserted itself and we have endured. In Deuteronomy the Lord speaks to the Israelites and what he says is roughly this: "Let it be recorded against you that I have set before you life and death, a blessing and a cursing. Therefore choose life that thou and thy children may live." We exercise that choice between life and death in the decisions we make each day. We must resolve that we will most often choose life and that which embellishes life. Me, I want to stick with the Israelites. One of these days is going to come and go and take me with it, and I don't want to depart feeling that I've wasted a minute of the precious stuff that life is made of. I want it all, and as it is, sad and gay and tragic and funny and triumphant.

Somehow, and with no particular evidence to support the supposition, I believe that we will be all right. The dangers, the challenges, the gigantic problems that face us in the immediate future may, if we have a little bit of luck, galvanize us into a new solidarity, a new growth, an awakening of our better selves. Crisis sometimes brings out the best in us. When countries are threatened by an invader, the people find in themselves the hidden resources and the strength that survival demands. Our enemies now have abstract names, but the threat is no less real, and our response may be in keeping with the need.

I cannot believe that life has become so impersonal and inhuman that it can crush the hardy and lusty spirit that has brought us to this time and place, not now when the centuries are piled so high, not when we've survived so many disasters before.

I will not believe that the brutality of the times can crush the eagerness, the buoyancy, the enthusiasm, the appetite that I see in the shining and expectant faces of my sons. I will not accept that we are so small of stature or confused of mind or shallow in spirit that we will allow anything to snuff out that delight in being alive, that desire to know all, the incredible hunger in their eyes, the ceaseless beauty in their voices, those voices that are talking always, rehearsing their knowledge, giving form to thoughts, playing with words, turning them upside down and all around, experimenting, tasting, feeling, absorbing. All that has to be indestructible, as man is indestructible, as the family is indestructible.

I want them to grow into honorable men. Certain helpful words have been cheapened by our wrongful usage of them. "Honor" is such a word. We have talked about achieving honor when we meant winning prizes. We have talked about peace with honor when we meant saving face. Once when we spoke of a man of honor, it meant a person of high-minded character or principles, with a fine sense of his obligations. An honorable man was an upright man, a man of worth, of dignity, moral integrity, and noble purpose. I hope that my sons will live with honor in a world that is not afraid to use such a word and respect such a concept.

It is up to me to give my children the chance they deserve. I must create for them not a cocoon of security in which they can hide but a shelter in which they can gird themselves; provide them with a world in which they can use their own wide-open eyes, develop wills of their own, learn to judge and evaluate, and make decisions. I must see that they do not lose their gift of laughter. There is more music in the laughter of one child than in all the poems of all the poets who ever lived, more sunshine than in a century of summers.

If you and I can come close to this in our own families, it will be the most important thing we will ever have done in our lives.

Life itself is brief, and yet each life encloses all eternity. We are, all of us, separately and together, engaged on the same tough journey. Each of us alike tastes of its joys and its sorrows. Each of us gets by as best he can. And we must, whenever possible, reach out to each other, tentatively to touch, with our hands, with our eyes, and with our hearts. We must wish for each other love and laughter, smiles and sunshine, good thoughts and happy days.

We must go rejoicing in the blessings of this world, chief of which is the mystery, the magic, the majesty, and the miracle that is life.

WYATT COOPER was born on a farm in Quitman, Mississippi, in 1927, was graduated from high school in New Orleans, and attended the University of California in Berkeley, and U.C.L.A., where he majored in theatre arts. He has been an actor on stage and in television, a screenwriter, and an editor. He is married to the artist Gloria Vanderbilt, and they live in New York with their two sons, Carter and Anderson.